Praise for *The Craving*

"A remarkable achievement. Dr. Ruden has managed to articulate a simple and elegant model that explains far-reaching aspects of human behavior, most notably the devastating problem of addiction. This will provide the impetus for study and investigation for years to come."

—David M. McDowell, M.D.,
New York State Psychiatric Institute,
Columbia University College of Physicians and Surgeons

"Dr. Ruden's approach to addiction is informative, elegant, and a pleasure to read. It is clear he has mastered a difficult, often murky field which will hopefully aid many of our patients and provide new pathways for research."

—Douglas Marcus, M.D.,
senior attending physician,
South Oakes Hospital, Amityville, New York

THE CRAVING BRAIN

THE CRAVING BRAIN

A BOLD NEW APPROACH TO BREAKING FREE FROM •DRUG ADDICTION •OVEREATING •ALCOHOLISM •GAMBLING

Second Edition

RONALD A. RUDEN, M.D., Ph.D.,
with MARCIA BYALICK

Perennial

An Imprint of HarperCollins*Publishers*

HarperCollins books may be purchased for educational, business, or sales promotional use. For information please write: Special Markets Department, HarperCollins Publishers Inc., 10 East 53rd Street, New York, NY 10022.

FIRST PERENNIAL EDITION PUBLISHED 2000.

Designed by Joseph Rutt

Library of Congress Cataloging-in-Publication Data is available.

ISBN 0-06-092899-9

00 01 02 03 04 ❖/RRD 10 9 8 7 6 5 4 3 2 1

To my wife and my daughter, Jackie and Jamie,
for whom I hope never to lose my addiction

CONTENTS

▼ CONTENTS ▼

PREFACE

The ideas presented here began to germinate in July of 1992 with the publication of Michael Weintraub's article on the use of two medications for the treatment of obesity. These medications altered brain neurochemicals that appeared to affect appetite. To be fair, my interest was driven by Gina Kolata's *New York Times* article describing this work. As I began to use the Weintraub protocol, it became clear that weight loss was only part of what these medications were accomplishing. What was astonishing about Weintraub's work was not so much that weight loss could be achieved, but the fact that while on these medications the weight loss could be maintained. In addition, patients reported a loss of their cravings and an overall sense of well-being.

As a medical nutritionist for more than a decade, I had seen patients lose weight on any number of diet programs, then watched them struggle to maintain their weight loss. The ability of overweight individuals to accept chronic food deprivation at levels as low as four hundred calories a day for extended periods of time has never ceased to amaze me. Nor has the sad reality that most of them regained their lost weight. A significant number have undergone this process repeatedly.

Why couldn't obese individuals stay on a diet? Over the years, some patients told me that they just couldn't stop themselves. Others said they just ate mindlessly, often not knowing what they were eating. The common belief that eating is controllable has led us to expect people "to behave" or pay the price of public shame. But diets don't work; eating too much is not due to a lack of willpower. Eating, ultimately, is under the control of the brain.

Hunger makes us seek and eat food. It is one of life's most powerful forces. That this drive is inherent and controlled by the brain is well documented. You eat, you get full, you get hungry sometime in the future. This is our appetitive drive. Some people have big appetites, others small appetites. Some people leave food on their plates, others eat food on other people's plates. Some people get hungry again quickly, others can't look at food for a long time. Everyone is different, but everyone remains the same. If we want to control food intake, we must use our minds to resist signals of hunger sent by our brains. Maintaining weight loss by dieting requires a continuous conscious effort to eat less. Like our inability to eventually resist sleep, our brains will override our minds and make us eat. This is in the nature of any living organism where the brain dictates survival behavior.

It is difficult to imagine eating food without being hungry. However, among many of my overweight patients, eating when not hungry and being unable to control their food intake is a common thread. For these individuals, compulsive eating was preceded by obsessional thoughts about food. Is obesity then partly an obsessive-compulsive disorder that leads to increased food intake? If this is true, it would explain current data in the weight-control industry. New diet books are successful because each provides a new obsessional focus for the hopeful buyer. But brain-driven obsessive thoughts of food eventually override obsessive thoughts of the diet program. Non-hunger eating returns, and the weight is regained.

In January of 1995, I was contacted by Dr. Pietr Hitzig, who was also using this protocol and had written about its use in alcoholism. His ideas fell on fertile ears. It was from our early discussions that the ideas presented here began to germinate. I am in his debt for initiating my thinking along these lines. As I understood his ideas, in those patients suffering from alcoholism the neurochemicals dopamine and serotonin were not in the correct proportion to each other, nor were their levels adequate. Accordingly, by raising and balancing them, one could stop alcohol cravings. In addition, he believed that a variety of ailments, including immune diseases, fibromyalgia, and emotional illnesses such as depression, could be treated this way.

My focus remained on food and addiction. A breakthrough in my thinking came while I was trying to understand why we needed different support groups for each problem. Why did we need an Alcoholics Anonymous for alcohol, an Overeaters Anonymous for compulsive eaters, and a Gamblers Anonymous for gamblers? Why couldn't there just be an Addictions Anonymous? It was also unclear why, more often than not, individuals who successfully followed these programs gained weight and increased their cigarette and coffee consumption. For certain individuals, solving one problem seemed to lead them to yet another addiction. The answer literally came to me in a "Eureka" sort of way while I was walking alone in my backyard. I screamed and jumped up and down. I couldn't sleep that night as I began to develop the concepts that would lead to a unified theory of addiction.

This book traces the origins of addictive behavior to prehistoric times before man strode on this planet. It outlines a new theory of mind that allows us to explain the interaction of the forces of nature and nurture in setting the stage for the craving response. The book concludes with approaches to solving this problem and where responsibility lies. The ideas presented here are a theory. A good theory explains many things. A great theory leads to new investigations with a new view. And every theory must stand the test of time and scrutiny.

There are many wonderful people who have been helped with this approach. They were the early pioneers, and I am indebted to all of them. Some volunteered their time to tell their stories. We have respectfully changed their names, but not their words.

This book is about biology as told through the lives of those who suffer from addictive behavior. We have written the first six chapters for the reader who wants to understand the roots of addiction and how we approach this problem. The section titled "The Scientific Foundation" explores these ideas via the primary scientific literature and is intended for those who wish to understand the science of biobalance. This is not a self-help book. Instead, its intent is to bring to the general public a new way of looking at this very old problem. A glossary is included and the words we chose to define are italicized the first time they are mentioned. We hope this work will open new avenues for discussion and research and presage the end of addiction.

ACKNOWLEDGMENTS

I want to express my gratitude to the scientists and researchers who provided the richly detailed field of science from which this theory was harvested. In particular, I must mention Dr. Pietr Hitzig for sharing his approach to solving the problems of addiction. I'd like to acknowledge those individuals who battle valiantly against addictions. In our culture this struggle is still imbued with shame. I hope this book eases some of their pain. I want to thank Carol Tannenhauser for her help in writing early parts of this book. I happily acknowledge my debt to Jason Kaufman and the venerable Larry Ashmead, my editors at HarperCollins. It was Larry who thought there was a book in me and offered to help find it.

But most of all I appreciate the many friends and patients who listened to my theory as it developed during the last several years. In particular, Cary Bunin, David Linker, and Vera Vento, whose help was crucial in putting me to the task of making sure everything made sense. These three logged literally hundreds of hours hearing my voice and I am thankful for their continuing friendship. A major thank you to Marcia Byalick, whose infinite patience, skill, and talent helped me complete this book.

The commitment of my partner in life and wife, Jacalyn Barnett, to me and to this endeavor was critical. She edited manuscripts, listened endlessly as this project evolved, made our house into a home, and all the while ran a major law practice. She is astonishing, and I am, as always, grateful for her love and support.

PREFACE AND ACKNOWLEDGMENTS TO THE SECOND EDITION

When fenfluramine was shown to cause heart problems, the use of drugs to biobalance the brain became considerably less appealing. My interest was then drawn to the neurofeedback work by Peniston. One of his articles listed the name of the company which made the devices he first used to treat alchoholism. I called the company and spoke to its president, Adam Crane. Over the course of a year Adam guided my understanding of neurofeedback. He also introduced me to Kara Alexander, a neuroscientist and computer wiz who joined in the development of the ideas presented here. I am grateful to these individuals for listening to, commenting on, and adding to my intellectual wanderings.

▼   ▼   ▼

This edition describes the use of neurofeedback for the treatment of alcoholism. We offer an explanation of its effect and propose an approach which potentially leads to a cure. In neurofeedback we are training the brain. Conceptually, being able to train neuronal functioning voluntarily makes sense, as it occurs when we gain any new skill (like playing the piano).

Since other organs are paced and sustained by their own, inherent electrical activity (the heart, the intestine, our musculoskeletal system) it makes sense to explore what governs the electrical activity of the brain. A brain model for the new millenium will need to be an electrochemical one, and it will generate new ideas about the mystery that makes us who we are.

THE
CRAVING
BRAIN

This book is written as a reference source only. It is not intended to be a substitute for the advice of the reader's personal physician or medical professional, whose advice should be sought before beginning any treatment suggested by this book. All efforts have been made to ensure the accuracy of the information contained in this book as of the date published. The author and the publisher expressly disclaim responsibility for any adverse effects arising from the use or application of the information contained herein.

1

▼

SURVIVAL

"Gotta have it" is the driving thought of an addict. "Gotta have it." A drink, a drag, a hit, a line, a pill, another piece of chocolate. "Gotta have it." Getting it is all that matters. Scrounging in the garbage for cigarette butts, stealing pills from a friend's medicine chest, driving into a dangerous neighborhood at night to meet a drug dealer, wiping out a child's bank account. Nothing is more important than smoking, swallowing, snorting, shooting, somehow securing and consuming it, and feeling its effects, *now*. Not health or physical safety. Not love or work or sex or money or relationships or responsibility. Not commitment or common sense or self-respect. Not the law or the truth. This urgent inner demand overrides all others, undermines reason, resolve, and will. It is relentless. It does not stop until it is satisfied. And then, it starts again. "Gotta have it!" What drives this madness?

"It's not the physical withdrawal," Tom Krause insists. "It's the craving that kills you." With his blond hair and blue eyes, button-down collar and crewneck sweater, he looks more like the quintessential college boy back in town for his twenty-fifth reunion than the hard-core codeine addict he was until four months ago. "I can take physical pain," he says. "I'm an athlete. I've had plenty of injuries and broken bones. I've handled *withdrawal* so many times it's absurd. I can take stomach cramps. I can take my head feeling like it's in a vice. What I can't take is standing in the shower at seven o'clock in the morning thinking I'm okay, and all of a sudden, out of the clear blue sky, I'm saying, 'I have to buy a drug.' The next thing I know, I'm calling my dealer. I could walk out of an NA meeting feeling great and three blocks later say, 'I gotta have a drug.' Where does that come from?"

What perversion of our instincts for self-preservation and independence spawns such powerful and self-destructive dependency? How does it develop and why in some people and not in others?

"In college, honest to God, I never even took a drink," Tom continues. "That's how serious I was about sports. I played football and baseball. I was an all-American, if you can believe that. When I got out of graduate school in the mid sixties, I smoked grass for the first time. And I liked it. Then I understood what people meant by a 'mind-altering' drug. I thought it was terrific. Everybody was doing it—not everybody, but eighty percent. I've got friends—guys who are running companies now—who were smoking marijuana every day before they went to work. They stopped, and I kept going, switching from drug to drug."

What compels someone to cross the line from user to abuser to addict? Why can one person have a drink or two and feel satisfied, while another keeps drinking until the bottle is empty? Why, for some, does eating, one of life's most basic needs, become all-consuming? Why do different people get addicted to alcohol and others to cigarettes?

Why do some find barbiturates, painkillers or heroin, cocaine or chocolate more appealing? Is the answer in the abused substance or the substance abuser? What, if anything, do they have in common with activities like exercise, gambling, shopping, work, and sex when they are pursued compulsively? Are they *addictions*, too? And finally, where do the roots of the addiction lie: in our genes or our environment; in our chemistry or our character?

"I know my psychiatrist thought I had some kind of moral defect," Tom reveals ruefully. "He would say, 'You're too impatient. Tough it out. It will get better.' But it didn't. So he'd tell me to do the NA thing, take it hour by hour. That's easy to say. There are twenty-four hours in a day, every day. You miss one of those hour-by-hours, and you're right back! I toughed it out for eighty-seven days once before I called him and said, 'If you don't write me a prescription, I'm going to get it illegally, because I can't take this anymore.' He said, 'You are babying yourself, Tom. You have to develop a higher threshold to pain.' So what happens? Your self-esteem goes down even more. You think, 'Oh my God, a shrink can't help me. NA can't help me. A clinic can't help me. I've tried them all and I'm still failing. What's wrong with me?' That on top of the physical stuff, on top of the 'I-gotta-have-the-drug I-want-the drug'—it's too much. You're going to lose all the time."

Obsessive thoughts, the inability to resist and the inability to stop, accompanied by feelings of powerlessness and inadequacy are the elements of individual stories of addiction, no matter what the substance or activity involved.

Sandy Scopek, a married woman in her forties and the mother of two teenage girls, echoed and amplified Tom's words. Sandy's substance of abuse is food, an even more insidious and difficult choice to understand. It is the constancy, intensity, and insatiability of her urge to eat that set Sandy apart.

"If I'm in the kitchen, I have to eat something," she says. "If I'm walking down the street and I pass a grocery store, I have to go in and buy some candy. When I come out, I'll have a pretzel on the corner and a hot dog on the next corner. If I go out to dinner and there are eight pieces of bread on the table, I'll eat six of them. If the hors d'oeuvres are being passed around at a party, I'm running after them. It's humiliating! Not just the fact that I crave food so badly, I can't even control it in front of other people. It isn't a hunger issue. I can be full, and ten minutes later I'm stuffing something else into my mouth. It's as if someone else is bending me to their will. No amount of discipline or strength can stop the craving. It's on my mind all the time.

"But this isn't about being thin," Sandy insists. "First of all, I'm not fat. I've never been fat. I've fluctuated between forty to sixty pounds overweight all my life. Of course, I'd rather be thin. I know I look better when I weigh less, but honestly, that isn't the issue. It's the compulsion. It's the slavery. It's the feeling that you can't help it, and no one understands why, and no one believes you. My husband is one of those truly disciplined, self-controlled people. He would say, 'Oh, yes, I understand, but you know, Sandy, if you can just eat a little less you probably wouldn't have this problem.' They think, 'Look what she's doing to herself. We're in control of our lives. If she really wanted to change, she could. Therefore, she must like the way she is, or else she's really weak.' It's very upsetting and demoralizing. You sit down and think, 'What am I in for, for the rest of my life? Am I always going to be eating this way? Are people always going to be looking at me disapprovingly or patronizingly or pityingly. Why can't I stop?'"

Ultimately, for Sandy and Tom, it is impossible to override their most fundamental drive . . . to survive. Gotta have it—or perish—is the message that the brain sends out. Perish without a piece of cake? Without a fifth drink? Yes. Ancient biology underlies their behavior. That "gotta have it" message races along neural pathways hardwired into the brain hundreds of millions of years ago, designed to ensure that the organism it inhabits continues to exist. No thought, no intention, and no consequences are involved. When this system developed, no parts of the brain capable of such sophisticated cognitive functions had yet evolved. The "mind" was still millennia away. There was only the "old brain," the one we have in common with reptiles, rodents, snakes, snails, and every other organism that has managed to survive on this demanding and dangerous planet.

This message was sent only when the organism had to be motivated to act in the interest of its own survival or the survival of its species. To accomplish this, nature designed internal systems to sense and monitor our bodies. By altering the levels of substances called *neurochemicals* and *glucocorticoids*, these systems brought our perceived needs to our immediate attention. If the need became life-threatening and our survival depended on the performance of a certain behavior, these systems made our thoughts involuntary and irresistible. Actions had to be taken . . . or we'd perish.

In the case of addiction, abnormal levels of these substances appear to sustain the individual in a perpetually activated state, a survival mode. Highly responsive to *stimuli*, much of it well below conscious awareness, we react as if our lives are at stake. Understanding how and why this occurs could provide a way of treating addiction. We therefore begin our story by first exploring the elegant and extraordinarily effective *survival system* devised by nature eons ago, when life on Earth began.

IN THE BEGINNING

Why are we here?

Philosophy yields to biology.

We are here because we survived. We each survived because we made it through gestation and the birth canal into the care of people who, whatever their strengths or short-comings, managed to feed and protect us. We survived because, as a group, science and society collaborated to shield us from diseases that a century ago would have killed us before we emerged from childhood. We survived as individuals by being fortunate enough to avoid both the natural and unnatural disasters that threaten us as we navigate the mine-field that is life.

In a broader sense, we are survivors because our parents survived, and theirs and theirs. We are survivors because our primate and reptilian ancestors survived, as did even our most ancient ancestors—insentient creatures, unaware of their own existence. We are survivors because Nature, the embodiment and force behind biology, endowed them all with traits and tools and miraculous mechanisms to make sure they got done what all living creatures must do to perpetuate their species: survive.

Consider Nature's challenge: Here were primitive creatures needing to be motivated to struggle to exist. Like a loving and generous parent, she provided each of them with the skills they needed. Some she gave size, some she gave speed, and some she gave strength. Some were given senses so acute they could detect sights, scents, and sounds from vast distances. She gave some beaks and teeth, shells and stingers, wings and hands. She gave some brilliant colors, coats, and combs. Some were camouflaged, others stood out.

Nature gave them all internal organs to effect bodily functions so that they could adapt to new environments. They were given vessels to carry blood and nutrients to the body and muscles to pump the blood and effect motion and strength. They were provided with mechanisms to consume, digest, and distribute food, to eliminate waste, regulate body functions, and stave off foreign invaders. Nature also gave them sleep to restore themselves. These organs and processes were placed under the control of regulator systems whose actions monitor and maintain our bodies. If, for example, we are outside and our body temperature drops, these systems act to warm us. We shiver and decrease blood flow to the extremities. Then, as our metabolic rate increases, our temperature returns to normal. Through the action of these regulator systems, Nature keeps the organism in a state of *homeostasis*, internally stable despite varying external conditions. Nature coordinated all of this via a central system, crowned with a brilliantly creative and effective organizing structure. She gave them each a brain.

Through the process of evolution, Nature adapted generation after generation of different species to their environment, keeping the most successful traits. Survival of the fittest was the mechanism of natural selection. Species evolved into new and often more complex species, refining but retaining the primitive structures and systems that served them well in earlier incarnations. The human brain is an example. Deep in its center lies the *limbic system*, known as the reptilian brain, which still performs functions necessary for survival much as it did for the creatures who preceded us by hundreds of millions of years.

The limbic system directs survival behaviors and initiates the gotta-have-it response. The three primal survival behaviors—eating, avoiding being eaten, and reproducing—are directed by this system. All have an active component, things we must do for ourselves to stay alive. Whether the behavior involves foraging in the forest for food or ordering dinner by telephone, climbing up a tree or double-locking the door, swimming upstream to spawn or squeezing into tight jeans, the system in the brain that drives these behaviors is the same. This ancient part of the brain gathers the sensory input necessary for survival. From there, bundles of nerve-cell fibers course their way to a cluster of nerve-cell bodies known as the nucleus accumbens. This structure also receives a large array of vital information from other parts of the brain. The incoming data about our internal and external environments as well as our emotional state and the relative importance of this information is processed here. It is the limbic system that tells us what we need. It is the nucleus accumbens, processing input from various parts of the brain, that produces the needed response . . . go and get it!

THE NUCLEUS ACCUMBENS

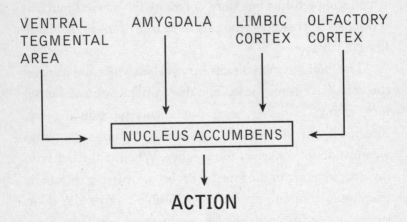

VENTRAL TEGMENTAL AREA IS INVOLVED WITH REWARDING ASPECTS OF BEHAVIOR.

AMYGDALA IS IMPLICATED IN THE EMOTIONAL AND MOTIVATIONAL ASPECTS OF BEHAVIOR.

LIMBIC CORTEX IS INVOLVED WITH SELF AND SPECIES PRESERVATION.

OLFACTORY CORTEX IS INVOLVED WITH OUR BODY'S RESPONSE TO ODORS.

The nucleus accumbens serves as an integration center that takes all the information and sends a motivational signal to other parts of the brain to carry out the needed task. As we'll see, understanding how this is accomplished for the three primal survival behaviors—getting food, finding a safe place, and having sex—will lead us to a solution for preventing addictive behavior.

HUNGER IS NOT DEBATABLE

For mammals, the critical systems necessary for survival are activated the instant the child is separated from its umbilical cord. Survival is now, to some extent, its own responsibility. With the trauma of birth behind him, no longer fully and automatically sustained by his mother, the newborn must face challenges as a separate entity. Conscious awareness is not necessary, nor is knowledge, mobility, or strength. All behavior is driven from within by survival systems sending information to the nucleus accumbens. Even at this stage, the most unknowing and helpless of creatures, the human infant, must do something to play a role in determining his own fate. In order to survive, he must learn to express his needs to someone who can answer them. Nature chose pain, as both a motivator and instructor.

Consider first the primal need for food. After birth, the body's survival system designed to get food is called into action. In biological terms, receptors throughout the body sense that nourishment is needed. Various chemical levels fluctuate and homeostasis is disturbed. That information is sent to the brain by messengers called transmitters. When the brain receives these signals, it produces growling noises in the stomach and then pain. The pain makes the infant cry. The mother's breasts are full and aching. She hears the cry, and milk enters her mammary glands, increasing her discomfort. The union of the mother's nipple and the baby's mouth relieves both of them. It doesn't take a baby long to learn that as a result of his mother's appearance, he will not only be relieved of pain, but he'll be comforted by the memory of the peace and contentment he felt when he drank that delicious milk, was held by his mother, and the pain disappeared. His mother also experiences relief from her pain, as well as peace and contentment. The maternal bond is made. The infant gets fed. Nature's survival system is successful.

But getting something to eat isn't always a priority. If we are busy and distracted by our current situation, these messages may never reach consciousness. Or we may realize we are hungry, but put it out of our minds. However, because getting food is a survival issue, our survival system continues to send signals that will get stronger with time. Eventually, despite our best efforts, we'll be unable to stop thinking about getting some food to stop the pain. We'll eat and then return to whatever we were doing. This illustrates our survival system at work.

Let's take a look at what our ancestors experienced when

food wasn't available. Someone had to go out and find it, kill it, or collect it. Not only were periods of famine common, but our early predecessors had to compete for food against larger, more powerful predators. The possibility also existed that they, too, could become someone's meal. There must have been times when they were tired and scared. They needed to be motivated to go out and get food. The pain produced by the primal survival system for food must have been intense. There was no arguing with these feelings. Our ancient forefathers knew that in order to stop the pain, they needed to get food.

HOME IS WHERE THE HERD IS

The pain produced by the brain motivates beings to struggle. It is the teacher in the survival system. The same method is used to help prevent us from becoming the victims of predators and, for the most part, keep us out of trouble. The brain is taught to respond to two types of beings: predator and not predator. It also understands two circumstances: safe and dangerous. It is crucial to survival that the individual be able to make these distinctions.

The animal senses potential danger. It could be that he sees a strange shadow, hears the unexpected snap of a twig, or detects an unknown scent. His brain is alerted and pain, in the form of anxiety, is created. He must respond to reduce this discomfort. He must either find a safe place or identify these sensations as coming from a friendly source. This will remove his anxiety and bring peace and contentment.

This primal security system is not concerned with the kind of acute, life-threatening events that inspire raw terror and cause a creature to shift into the biological mode known as "fight or flight." Those reactions are driven by a different survival system and a different biochemical response is produced. The security survival system focuses on the everyday social arrangements and contact. For us, it is activated by the stresses of everyday life, by concerns like job security, health problems, and relationship issues.

How do animals reduce their anxiety and remove their pain? For the most part, animals band together. The idea that there is safety in numbers comes not from the fact that there are others who will likely be killed before you. Rather, it is our internal sense that when those around us are like us, we are safe. Nature, by and large, has taught us that we do not kill our own kind. What produces this comforting feeling of "us"? It is a process driven by *pattern recognition*. Herding is a powerful animal instinct. It clearly and profoundly decreases the pain and anxiety produced by the survival system for safety. As observed by the nineteenth-century naturalist Francis Galton:

> The ox . . . cannot endure even a momentary severance from his herd. If he be separated from it by stratagem or force, he exhibits every sign of mental agony; he strives with all his might to get back again

and when he succeeds, he plunges into its middle, to bathe his whole body with the comfort of close companionship.

From birth, sights, smells, sounds, and the patterns of our environment let us know that in the confines of the herd we are not the object of someone's hunger. The herd is comfort and contentment. This feeling of safety allows one to eat and mate. From colonies of wasps to schools of fish, from herds of wildebeests to gaggles, prides, flocks, and packs, herding makes us feel at home. It is the feeling engendered by everyday suburban living, religious organizations, country clubs, and ethnic neighborhoods. Indeed, home and safety is where the herd is. This *primal survival system* instills an all-important sense of belonging that, as you will see, plays an important role in the treatment of addictive disorders.

GETTING AND BEGETTING

The third survival system is directed toward one purpose: procreation. For more complex species, procreative sex is not only directed toward continuing the species, but improving it as well. How is this motivated?

This primal survival system makes us want to have sex. Here again, Nature teaches and motivates us with pain. Although we derive pleasure from touching our genitals beginning at infancy, the desire for sex, the "gotta have it," the pain, begins at puberty. Biologically, the onset of adolescence is characterized by a rise in the pubertal hormones *estrogen* and *testosterone*. Behaviorally, it is a tumultuous time.

Teenage years are few in the total life cycle, but they are critical in the maturation process. Behaviors fueled by the hormones in our bodies lead to increased aggression, acts of rebellion, and the especially powerful desire for sex. The drive manifests itself in many ways. Adolescents provide sexual signals in the clothes they wear, the way they dance, and the language they use. These signals involuntarily increase sexual desires. The resultant sexual thoughts, the throbbing in our loins, and the relentless preoccupation with wanting to have sex are painful. Clearly, these feelings just begin at puberty. The course of history has been altered time and again by the overwhelming desire for people to have sex.

To be operational, this survival system requires the presence of these sex hormones. While their main function is to drive the desire for sex, we will see that they are also critical for the acquisition of addictive behavior.

SURVIVAL BEHAVIOR

How does Nature accomplish this task? Where do the primal survival systems derive their power to motivate behavior? The symptoms generated by these survival systems are painful. The pain of hunger, anxiety, and longing create *stress*, focus our attention, and disturb homeostasis.

The brain is altered. The greater the need, the greater the pain. The greater the pain, the greater the stress. The power to move us to action is generated in the nucleus accumbens. Upon appropriate stimulation from various brain structures, the nucleus accumbens releases a neurochemical called *dopamine*, which sends the signal to act. The amount of dopamine released depends on the intensity of the stress. The greater the stress, the greater the rise in dopamine. The faster and greater the rise in dopamine, the more powerful the response.

Dopamine is a primitive molecule. Derived from the simple amino acid phenylalanine, it is found throughout the body performing a variety of functions such as regulating blood flow, adjusting hormone levels, and setting the timing of the movement of the intestines. But its most central roles, and the ones that concern us here, are those essential for survival. They include dopamine's ability to focus our attention and activate behavior. Dopamine increases our ability to focus our senses and aids in learning. On a day-to-day basis, dopamine, in parts of the brain outside the nucleus accumbens, appears to increase the level of arousal and make us more alert. It is the chemical in command when you down a dozen cups of coffee. It is dopamine that heightens awareness, helps us prioritize our senses, and dilates our pupils. Dopamine is also necessary for learning those responses needed for survival. In an emergency, it is converted to adrenaline, the chemical we rely on in life-threatening situations.

Dopamine levels rise in the nucleus accumbens during effort, the *anticipatory* (the "getting it") *phase of goal-driven behaviors*. They are at their highest when an animal is actively seeking food, a safe place, or a mate. These levels are elevated, for example, when squirrels are foraging for food or when we hear that a big snowstorm is coming and we rush to stock up on milk and toilet paper. We can't easily say no to dopamine's commands.

But what is it that makes us feel safe, sated, and satisfied? What stops the behavior? It is another primitive molecule, *serotonin*. Derived from the simple amino acid tryptophan, serotonin is the soother, the quieter, the anti-impulsive agent. Serotonin constrains dopamine's actions. It decreases both our focus and our ability to make connections with other parts of the brain. It darkens the *landscape*, lowering recognition of like things. Serotonin is what we need when we are overwhelmed by too much at once.

Too little serotonin makes us irritable. Our annoyance threshold goes down, and we can be drawn into action in an instant. A low level of serotonin allows for so many connections to be made that too much becomes significant. Our thoughts either become obsessional or the brain becomes overloaded and can process nothing.

When one of the survival systems brings a need to our attention, it causes discomfort and thereby produces stress. Sensitivity to dopamine release in the nucleus accumbens is raised. Other areas of the brain also increase dopamine levels.

We are on the alert, ready to act. If we are unable to find food, a safe place, or a mate, the urgency increases. Serotonin levels decrease. At this point, we can't let the thought go. While the primal survival system drives us to seek food, safety, and sex, it is not until the serotonin drops low enough that the idea becomes obsessional. The uneasy combination of rising dopamine and lowered serotonin forces us to seek any solution to end this pain. It is as if a light emanating from the inner world is suddenly turned outward, making every pattern more salient. The drive to stop this longing becomes critical and clear. This is craving. Far from being pleasurable, it is uncomfortable. To decrease the stress, the reward must be the one the animal already knows will produce the desired results. If we don't accomplish these tasks, our pain becomes inescapable. We starve, get eaten, or never reproduce. The battle for survival is lost.

If dopamine is the "gotta have it," serotonin is the "got it." It is the rising dopamine that motivates us to action, and it is the attainment, the full belly, the safe place, the completed sexual act that raises serotonin. The brain is in a high dopamine and high serotonin state. Contentment floods our being. We feel safe, satisfied, and secure. The craving is gone. The ability of our brain to motivate the behavior is gone. We call this a *biobalanced* state. Understanding the biological process that produces this state will lead us to an approach to treat addiction.

We define the word *balance* in this context not in its com-

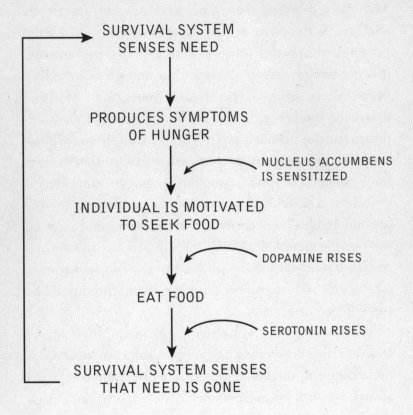

PRIMAL SURVIVAL SYSTEM FOR FOOD

SURVIVAL SYSTEM
SENSES NEED

↓

PRODUCES SYMPTOMS
OF HUNGER

NUCLEUS ACCUMBENS
IS SENSITIZED

↓

INDIVIDUAL IS MOTIVATED
TO SEEK FOOD

DOPAMINE RISES

↓

EAT FOOD

SEROTONIN RISES

↓

SURVIVAL SYSTEM SENSES
THAT NEED IS GONE

The survival system for food senses a need. Transmitters send the message to the limbic system, which produces feelings of hunger and causes stress. This increases the sensitivity of the nucleus accumbens. The seeking of food raises dopamine and the eating raises serotonin. The survival system senses that the need is satisfied and removes the pain of hunger, which reduces the sensitivity of the nucleus accumbens. The ability of food to motivate action is gone.

mon usage, as in seesaws or the scales of justice. Rather, the word balance implies harmony, a state of equilibrium. Neither pulled nor pushed, a balanced state means nothing more needs to be done. *Biobalance* refers to the feelings of contentment that nature has given us as the reward for our struggles. **It is the goal of motivated behavior.**

Why are so many motivated to seek out Jack Daniel's or Sara Lee, play poker or shoot heroin with a vengeance? These did not exist hundreds of millions of years ago when the primitive brain was designed. Neither did mankind. And why, as we search, do we exhibit the same gotta-have-it behavior designed by nature for use in critical survival situations? To find the answer, we must first look for the common thread that ties together all those who suffer from addiction.

2

▼

LANDSCAPING THE BRAIN

What do addicts look like? Do they have any identifying marks or traits? An addict can look like a tired social worker who treats battered women in New York. An addict can be an Olympic gold medalist, an army general, or a multimillion-dollar professional baseball player. An addict can look like the boy or girl next door. An addict can be French, English, Russian, Greek, Native American, African American, or any and every prefixed American. They are salespeople, lawyers, doctors, receptionists, mothers. They speak quickly, slowly, or not at all of their secrets, shame, lies, and self-destructiveness, of bottoming out, burning out, drying out, and pigging out. Often, it is only by their own admission that you know who are addicts.

While countless hours and research dollars have been expended trying to find out who will become an addict, no answer has been found. We can't stereotype addicts according to appearance, age, race, heritage, geography, religion, economic status, or temperament. Addiction transcends simple description. What is it then that ties all addicts together? Only that they exhibit addictive behavior. The fact that we cannot identify who becomes an addict causes us to recast our question in order to help direct us in our understanding. Instead, we ask: Why does someone become an addict?

"I knew something was wrong with me for a long time," Tom Sabatini says. "This has been going on for the better part of my life." By "this," Tom means a powerful pull toward and battle against all kinds of addictive behavior and mind-altering drugs—from the time he was twelve years old. It's not hard to imagine this about Tom. He is a big man and has a little craziness in his eyes. You get the feeling that he is like a bottle of champagne, thoroughly shaken, with the cork loose. Ironically enough, he works as a salesman with his brothers on systems that stabilize heavy machinery.

"Ten years old," he corrects. "Before I started drinking, I couldn't stop masturbating. That's a form of addiction, no doubt about it. I remember being thoroughly obsessed with it—if not masturbating, thinking about masturbating, all the time."

His wife, Susan, also an addict, met Tom at AA. They fell in love and got married. "I think my natural personality had something to do with it," Susan says, "but I didn't have to be this way. I wasn't doomed to be an addict." You can hear the not so little fear in her voice. The foundation of that fear was that her one-year-old son would suffer the same fate as his parents. "It has more to do with how I was raised and my situation."

Susan did have a rough time as a child. Her father died when she was four, and her mother was an alcoholic. She was left home by herself a lot and had tremendous fear of being alone in the house. With alcohol, the fear went away, and for the first time she felt connected with her friends. She always loved the taste of beer. "Maybe because I'm Irish." She laughs. Her courtship and marriage was punctuated by Tom's sometimes violent behavior.

"I was always loud," Tom says. "I couldn't sit still long enough to read a book. I was always moving around, looking for trouble, bragging about something. I was all ego and no self-esteem. I remember being very emotional, but of course I couldn't show that. My father and uncle would say, 'Real men don't cry, real men drink Jack Daniel's.' I was a scared little kid. I remember feeling fear running through my body. I was born in 1960. Some of my early memories are about the Vietnam War. Body counts, death, blood, it was terrifying. Bobby Kennedy's assassination. Writing to Martin Luther King's kids after he was killed. It was such a brutal time. I cried a lot to my dog, because I felt like I couldn't tell my family."

"Food was always a comfort to me," Tom says. Though clean now for four and a half months, he has gained forty pounds and is a chain-smoker. "At AA, we call what I'm doing switching seats on the *Titanic*," Tom adds wryly. "It doesn't matter what seat you are in, you're still going down."

Though he both drank and used heroin, Tom's drug of choice had been speed. "The first time I ever did speed I was sixteen years old," he says. Despite all the pain and loss he has subsequently endured, he seems to relish remembering. "Don't forget, I was a fat kid. I desperately wanted to get girlfriends. There was this quack who was prescribing 'black beauties.' My friend was going to him, and he said, 'Here, Tom, try one of these.' So I did. Now remember, when I was in high school in the early seventies, drugs were rampant. You could go up, down, or sideways, any way you wanted. I tried them all, but I never liked anything like I liked that first speed pill. Speed was my love. I would laugh at people who did downs, because they would be sloppy and stupid. Me, I could eat my speed and I felt like a king. I could do everything I couldn't do before. I could read, I could write. I could talk to women, men, teachers, anybody. I lost weight, girls loved me. Speed was what I wanted all along."

BEHAVIOR

For every animal, including humans, behavior originates at conception when luck and Nature choose our inherent abilities and disposition. The union of an egg with just one out of hundreds of millions of sperm ultimately creates a unique individual. Part of the biological entity is the terrain of the brain. The brain, like the face and torso, has its own unique features. It is through this terrain that the brain transforms what we sense and think into behavior. Our terrains dispose us to behave in a certain way. Susan Sabatini called it her "natural personality." In Tom's case, as you hear his life story, he was disposed to addictive behavior. It was in his nature.

What is terrain? We use the term *terrain* to describe the home of what is inherent. Some terrains produce deliberate, cautious, and friendly behavior; other terrains cause behavior that is impulsive, risk-taking, and aloof. No two terrains are alike, not even those of identical twins. Our terrain is truly the fingerprint of "who" we are and how we will respond to our environment. It's what some call temperament.

It has been repeatedly demonstrated that alcoholism runs strongly in families. Approximately one-third of alcoholics report having alcoholic parents. Research has revealed great differences in the rates at which individuals metabolize drugs, how sensitive they are to their effects, how quickly they develop *tolerance,* and how severe their withdrawal. There is evidence from adoption studies that even the children of alcoholics separated from their parents close to birth are at high risk for alcoholism. One study showed that if one twin of an identical set of twins developed alcoholism, there was a 60 percent chance the other twin also would. Clearly, what is inherited is important, but what about the other 40 percent?

Our experience profoundly alters our terrain, sometimes for short periods, sometimes for very long periods, sometimes permanently. Just as wind and rain change the surface of a pond, so do life's experiences shape our terrain into a landscape that predisposes our behavior. For the most part, when the wind and rain die down, we are left with the same pond. Our terrain, the essence of who we are, remains as well.

It is important to understand that some people's terrains are more vulnerable to the influences of their environments. Sometimes the same person can be more or less vulnerable to the same conditions. This reflects the biology of our inherent terrain. It is this complex mixture of interactions with the environment that alters our terrain and produces a dynamic, ever-changing landscape. As we shall see, it is this landscape that determines behavior. It is our landscape, then, that predisposes us to addictive behavior. Discovering what sort of landscape causes addictive behavior, how it develops and is sustained, will lead us closer to finding a solution for addiction.

AN ADDICTIVE TERRAIN

Not everyone uses drugs. Not everyone enjoys drugs. Not everyone who uses drugs becomes an addict. Some people can smoke two cigarettes a day, others need two packs. If drugs that are abused were all that was needed to cause addiction, everyone would be an addict. A sip of alcohol would lead to lifelong dependence. A lottery bet would lead to inveterate gambling and financial ruin. We'd all be compulsive eaters. Therefore, there must be something in our landscape that causes us to exhibit addictive behavior. For Tom Sabatini, his terrain required only a single contact with his drug of choice. "I never liked anything like I liked that first speed pill," he said.

An early human study on addiction under laboratory conditions found that for first-time heroin users, some liked it and some hated it. This simple experiment led to an approach that helps us understand what is inherent. It is called *preference drinking*. Although the complexity of human behavior precludes the straightforward analysis of the influences that lead to addictive behavior, laboratory rats have been bred to self-administer virtually all the drugs that are abused by humans. In these experiments, the animal is free to drink from two bottles, one containing the drug and the other containing water. Alcohol-preferring (P) rats could be bred for voluntary alcohol consumption simply by mating high-alcohol-consuming rats until there was a clear distinction between those bred to prefer alcohol and those bred not to prefer alcohol (NP). This selective breeding has provided the opportunity to study the biology of addictive behavior without the influence of the environment. It allows for the exploration of the difference in physiology and behavior between drinkers and nondrinkers.

Not only did the (P) rats prefer alcohol, they worked harder to get it, suggesting that somehow alcohol rewarded them. Indeed, they worked harder to obtain it even if alcohol was delivered by tube directly to their stomachs. Taste was not an issue. Research with these selected lines of rats suggests a role for lowered serotonin in parts of the brain. These studies were replicated for cocaine and *opiates* as well. In addition, when alcohol was given to the (P) rats, a greater release of dopamine in the nucleus accumbens was observed. While alcohol is known to interact with other brain systems, many pieces of evidence suggest that dopamine plays a central role in addictive behavior.

For the first time, we had two clues, at least in the animal model, that could possibly be used to help us understand human addiction. First, that the level of serotonin was low in these (P) animals and, second, that upon stimulation, their nucleus accumbens released more dopamine than those of the (NP) animals. The baseline levels of dopamine in the nucleus accumbens do not appear to play a role, nor do dopamine levels in other parts of the brain. These key observations provide the biological configuration of the addictive landscape. If an individual is born with this terrain, the risk for addiction is great. Do these results imply that all addictions are inherent? Or are there other forces that can landscape the terrain to predispose us to addictive behavior?

HORMONES AS LANDSCAPERS

One of the most dramatic and powerful forces to landscape our terrains and alter our behavior is puberty. It is so powerful that almost all cultures recognize it. Some even sanctify it, as in the Jewish ceremony of bar mitzvah. "Today, I am a man!" It is a time of passage, with both physical and emotional consequences. It is when hormones challenge our bodies and minds. Estrogen and testosterone complete the system that produces the pain of longing. These hormones lower serotonin levels and increase the sensitivity of the nucleus accumbens. Our minds lust and our bodies ache. We are motivated to have sex to remove the pain. Unfortunately, the primal survival system designed to drive sexual desires is not perfect. Having sex should quell the desire, but in our culture, we are discouraged from having sex until we are married, often well after adolescence. What happens when we can't have sex?

We are under stress, and other craving behavior occurs. As a consequence, adolescence is the time when many addictive and compulsive disorders begin. Bulimia and anorexia often surface during these years. It is a time when smoking cigarettes and drinking alcohol start. It is why we have laws to prevent teenagers from using alcohol. Plato knew what he was talking about when he said that "boys should abstain from all use of wine until the age of eighteen, for it is wrong to add fire to fire." This is indeed a challenging time, for estrogen and testosterone are powerful landscapers. Adolescent behavior ends only when the brain has adapted to these hormones.

Even after adolescence, we see the powerful influences of these hormones. The clichés of craving pickles and ice cream during early pregnancy when hormones are skyrocketing and the craving and emotional volatility before menstruation reflect the pervasive influences of estrogen on the landscape.

Thus it appears that our inherent terrain and how it is affected by our hormones can produce a landscape predisposed to addictive behavior. These are innate, inescapable processes that cannot be changed. We know that experience, our environment, our relationships, our feelings, and our thoughts can also alter our actions. They can alter our landscape and lead to addictive behavior. How this occurs requires an understanding of how our experiences landscape the brain.

EXPERIENCE AS A LANDSCAPER

All things are affected by their environments. Rocks worn by the wind and water produced the Grand Canyon. The global temperature drops and glaciers appear. Living things, however, respond to their environments. It is impossible to anticipate a behavioral response solely on what is perceived. We behave in certain ways because what we sense and perceive is processed on our landscape. It is our landscapes that direct our responses. The example outlined below shows that if we are happy and content, a minor annoyance, like someone cutting in front of us while we're driving, can be easily handled. If we are tired and angry, we may respond to the same situation with rage. Our blood pressure rises, our heart rate increases, our pupils dilate, and our hands grip the steering wheel tighter. We are ready for action. The identical *perception* of the event, someone cutting us off, yielded two different responses. Since our *sensation* and perception of the event were the same, it is our predisposition, our environmentally and hormonally modified terrain, our landscape, that directed our behavior.

Sensation	Perception	Predisposition	Response
Visual	Someone cuts us off	Content	Not important
Visual	Someone cuts us off	Frustrated	Anger

From an evolutionary point of view, our ability to respond to identical sensory input in different ways is critical to survival. Imagine if every time you saw food, you ate it. Or every time you saw a receptive sexual partner, you had to have sex right then and there. Our ability to get anything done would be dependent on avoiding any stimuli that would produce a response. This is almost impossible. Nature neatly solved this problem by giving our brains the capability of being altered so that perception won't always lead to the same response. Our environment landscapes the brain and allows us to adapt. It increases our chances of survival. How does this occur?

The sensory world we inhabit really has two parts: the *forefield*, which reflects that which is brought to conscious attention, and the *backfield*, that which remains *subconscious*. Taken together they form a *field*. It is this field that we continually sense and perceive. This perception is then processed on our landscapes. The *response* that is generated then activates behavior and conscious thoughts. It also produces physiological responses in the brain and body below *conscious* awareness.

It seems obvious that we will respond to what we are aware of. These responses can be brought to consciousness or remain subconscious. Seeing an attacker not only frightens us on the conscious level but also alters our physiology to engage in either fight or flight. Clearly, we respond to these forefield stimuli. But what evidence is there for backfield processes producing change? Can things that we are unaware of change our behavior and physiology? Classic psychotherapeutic concepts suggest that subconscious thoughts about past events can affect behavior. These events are thought to somehow affect the way we respond. Freudian theory suggests that it is only by bringing the subconscious to conscious awareness that the deleterious effects on our behavior can be addressed.

In summary, we postulate that it is not only past events both conscious and subconscious that affect behavior, but the ongoing daily exchange with the world we inhabit. This interaction affects the landscape and how we respond. Both forefield (conscious) perception and backfield (subconscious) perception can landscape the brain.

PATTERN RECOGNITION

Nature has surrounded us with such an amazing diversity of sights, sounds, tastes, touches, and smells. How is the brain to make sense of all this? The answer is through a pattern recognition process. Pattern recognition is the way in which the brain matches sensory input to create a perception. A perception is an interpretation of the *patterns* seen based on a set of rules. This perception is then molded by our current landscape and a response is generated. All responses begin with sensory input.

To bring sensory input to the forefield requires focus. For vision, it is looking directly at something, focusing the object on the macula lutea, where the highest concentration of light-receiving cells is found in the eye. For taste, which includes only salty, sweet, sour, and bitter, we roll food around our mouths. To bring sound to the forefield, certain animals have been given movable ears. We turn our heads and cup our ears with our hands so that we maximize incoming sound. For smell, we put the object under our noses and sniff. For our mind we bring a thought to our consciousness.

FOREFIELD PLACEMENT

SENSORY INPUT	MECHANISM
VISION	FOCUS ON MACULA
HEARING	TURNING OF EAR
SMELL	PLACE UNDER NOSE
TASTE	PLACE ON TONGUE
TOUCH	FEEL WITH FINGERTIPS
MIND	CONSCIOUS THOUGHT

Sensing leads to perception by a pattern recognition process. A plant is perceived because it has a stem, a flower, leaves, color, smell, and comes up from the ground. It is brought to consciousness (forefield) by focusing the appropriate sense (e.g., looking at the plant). This sensation is broken down into component parts and dispensed to areas of the brain where "vertical," "earth," "leaves," and "sweet smell" are located. Think of it as a scanning process. The brain matches these separated parts to patterns already stored in the brain. Once recognition occurs, that is, sufficient information is available for identification, it is somehow assembled and perception occurs. The perception is then processed on the current landscape, and if the object is in the forefield, it is brought to consciousness.

Scanning for connections allows for a piece of the flower to elicit the entire flower. We conceptualize this aspect of the brain as performing a matching function that is able to categorize sensation as patterns and then search for other patterns that are similar. This allows for all patterns to be perceived and interpreted. We often say that this looks or smells or tastes or feels like something else. We illustrate much of life with similes. Our brains actively seek familiar patterns in unfamiliar situations. Déjà vu occurs when many patterns overlap and recall another very similar situation. When the experience is unable to find a match, it becomes the unknown, and we feel anxious.

The same process occurs for backfield pattern recognition. The difference is that the patterns that the brain receives and scans for matches, and the perceptions that result, remain below consciousness. This perception is processed on our landscape and produces a response of which we are unaware. Despite this lack of awareness, the response can have profound effects on our behavior and physiology. There are many examples of this process. A relationship between the menstrual cycle and the lunar rhythm has recently been confirmed. The lunar rhythm is a backfield pattern. It was found that among 826 female volunteers with normal menstrual cycles, a large proportion of menstruations (28.5 percent) occurred around the time of the new moon. The portion of menstruations occurring at other times during the lunar month ranged between 8.5 and 12.5 percent. This reflects animal data in which the cycle of menses is tied to the lunar calendar. For humans, synchronization of menstrual cycles in women living together has been convincingly demonstrated. Researchers have found that it is some compound that is secreted from the underarms of menstruating females that sets the timing.

Our day-to-day backfield environment can produce profound biological changes. *Seasonal affective disorder*, the winter blues, reflects a backfield (subconscious) pattern recognition process involving the decreased amount of daylight that the brain experiences.

We experience backfield pattern recognition processing every day. For example, we leave a room to do a task, then forget what it was we were going to do. By returning to the room where we first thought of it, magically the task pops back into our consciousness. A pattern that we are unaware of produces a response just as surely as a hungry dog salivates when he sees food. Tom Krause, who inexplicably began craving his drug while in the shower, is another example. Thus, both forefield and backfield pattern recognition processes cause conscious and subconscious responses which then produce behavior.

The response to a perception is modulated by our landscapes. Our brains can improve the chances of finding matches by increasing the importance of the search. This also makes perfect sense from an evolutionary point of view. We want the things that are most significant to us to be readily recognized. The greater the ability to make matches, the greater the likelihood that the desired object will be brought to the forefield and action taken. When we are hungry, patterns that suggest food, such as scents and animal tracks, are more readily brought to conscious awareness. Just as we can increase the ability to make matches, the brain can also decrease this ability.

In summary, pattern recognition processing for both forefield and backfield leads to perception. The perception is processed through our landscapes and a response is produced. This response not only generates behavior, but alters the landscape as well. Thus for each response, a new landscape is formed. Most responses are short-lived, and the landscape returns to its baseline state when the pattern is no longer perceived. But in some cases, as we shall see, the changes are more permanent because the pattern recognition process is inescapable.

THE ORIGIN OF CHRONIC INESCAPABLE STRESS

That we are affected by our environment is clear. Our brain allows for a wide range of responses to what we experience. The pattern recognition process that causes anxiety, fear, hopelessness, despair, and sorrow might not be well understood, but the response they elicit is. They all produce stress. The stress can be mild or severe, internal or external, conscious or subconscious. It is often short-lived. It can be brought about by our thoughts and surroundings, our relationships or our bodies. If the stress is prolonged and change cannot occur, the individual, in order to improve chances of survival, must then adapt. It is the brain's ability to reduce the consequences of the stress, yet remain alert to solutions, that improves the chances for survival. It is this process that alters the landscape and predisposes us to addictive behavior.

As a stressful pattern is perceived and passes through the landscape, it produces a response. If the response provides a way to change the stress, the landscape returns to its baseline state. If we cannot change the stress, we adapt to the forefield pattern recognition. We become inured to garbage on the streets, noise in our environment, overcrowding in the subways. It becomes backfield. This process of adaptation, of bringing forefield pattern recognition to the backfield, has profound implications in addictive behavior. Forefield pattern recognition of distressful things produces action that motivates us to remove the stress. We look away, move away, or get out of the way. When this cannot happen, we place it in the backfield. These stressful things no longer reach consciousness. However, the perception of a stressful backfield pattern will still produce a response. This response will perpetuate this adaptation to our environment and further remove the stress from consciousness. If the stress is inescapable and pervasive, our landscape is altered. The way we respond to subsequent forefield and backfield patterns will be changed.

THE STRESS OF LIFE

Our response to stress and its effects on us have been well documented. Whether we are hungry or cold, worried about our debts or concerned about a loved one, we are under stress. The pioneering work of Hans Selye, the great Canadian physician and researcher, showed that acute stress produced an alarm reaction that caused a rise in substances called glucocorticoids. These substances reduce the effect of stress on the body and increase the body's ability to respond to novel or stressful situations. Glucocorticoids increase the sensitivity of the nucleus accumbens to release dopamine. When this occurs, we are more likely to be motivated by the stimuli around us. It increases our ability to respond to perceived solutions. However, if the stress is prolonged and inescapable, the levels of glucocorticoids diminish, but never return to the prestress baseline. Despite appearing to adapt to its environment, the nucleus accumbens, that structure through which survival responses are generated, remains sensitized. This allows for heightened action on a moment's notice.

Chronic stress and the consequent alteration of the landscape occur when the pattern recognition process appears inescapable. Suburban housewives who feel as if they've lost their purpose in life when their children leave home, as well as women trapped in welfare without the skills necessary to obtain employment, experience chronic inescapable stress. Lack of control is *inescapable stress*. Anxiety is inescapable stress. Dishonor is inescapable stress. Chronic illness is inescapable stress. A bad marriage can be inescapable stress. A childhood with abusive parents is inescapable stress. And addiction, in a self-perpetuating way, is inescapable stress. Data from animal studies suggest that chronic stress lowers serotonin levels. This landscape, a combination of low serotonin and a sensitized nucleus accumbens, is identical to both that found in (P) rats and the one produced as a consequence of estrogen and hormones.

"My goal in life is to help others who are still in the situation I finally climbed out of," Danielle begins softly. "For years, I thought what happened to me was my fault. The cops, neighbors, priests . . . nobody helped."

Danielle, a pretty but worn-looking forty-year-old who works in a shelter for battered women, began to tell her story. She grew up in Coney Island, a tough, working-class neighborhood in Brooklyn. Her first thirteen years were spent enjoying the beach and the boardwalk, bolstered by a vibrant sense of community and strong moral code. A good student, she had friends and a particularly warm relationship with her father.

"He was a short-order cook. Although he worked six and a half days a week, he always made me feel special. I have no memory of his ever criticizing me. When I was thirteen, I found him dead on the floor with his head split open on New Year's Eve. He had a heart attack and hit his head on the radiator when he fell down.

"From that moment on, my life changed. My mother was English. She always thought I was a little too independent, not ladylike enough. After my father died, she immersed herself in religion. She became a Jehovah's Witness, and that was the end of Thanksgiving and Christmas. Suddenly, any pleasure was pagan and evil. I couldn't be good enough. As the time went by, she really got fanatic. On the weekends, she made me go door-to-door giving out Jehovah's Witness pamphlets to our neighbors. I never really understood what the stuff said, but I knew that the neighbors were really turned off.

I'll never forget that feeling of humiliation. Remember, I was just thirteen or fourteen. I was without my father and all I wanted to do was fit in.

"Then it got worse. I was starting high school and she wouldn't let me wear short skirts or lipstick. This was the late sixties, and I stood out like a sore thumb. I went from a confident kid to one with low self-esteem in a matter of months."

For the young adolescent, struggling with typical young adult problems is hard enough. However, to live in a home where self-expression is prohibited, and physical and emotional abuse becomes a daily event, fills the criterion for chronic inescapable stress. Her landscape was changed.

"One day she whacked me in the back of the head with a frying pan because I spilled some milk in the refrigerator. Another morning, she decided she hated my long hair so she wrapped it around her hand, took scissors, and cut it all off, leaving a huge bald spot on the back of my head. Then she pushed me out the door to school.

"I started hanging out on weekends with kids from the local Catholic School. They didn't know my mother or see what I had to wear all week. And they drank beer. The beer made me feel good. It didn't take long for me to realize that when I drank, I didn't have to think about anything. My mother could beat me, I didn't care. At least if she was going to hit me, I would know what I had done to deserve it. The alcohol made me feel like I belonged. I liked feeling numb, I liked feeling brave enough to answer her back."

Soon after high school, Danielle married an alcoholic. She was beaten, raped, and forced to leave any job she held because her husband disapproved of her working. Her friends disappeared. She continued to drink until she was more often drunk than sober. This nightmare continued for twenty-five years, until she woke up in the hospital after a suicide attempt.

Inescapable fear, pain, and low self-esteem are all elements that cause our brains to adapt to the situation and set the stage for addictive behavior. Danielle's stress was inescapable from the time her father died. But inescapable stress does not have to be directed at us personally. It can also occur as a result of inescapable stress that is due to backfield pattern recognition.

The Native American Indians, once a great people so in harmony with nature, have been devastated by alcoholism. What kind of stress can explain this epidemic? Why has this persisted? The Indian nations are strangers living in a strange land. Stress that leads to substance abuse comes from the sense of not belonging, of not feeling safe. Today, we have terms to define their alienation. Acculturation stress results from the demands to integrate into and identify with another more dominant culture that *looks* different. Deculturation stress is that resulting from the loss or devaluation of historical tradition. Both can be classified as chronic inescapable stress. The situation in which the Indians found themselves was described by L. A. Heib in his review of Native American Indians.

Two hundred years ago, several thousand Seneca Indians lived in the Southwest portion of New York State. The Seneca tribes had a social structure with gender roles well defined. Men hunted, went to war, and were diplomats to neighboring tribes. The women managed the village, supervised the growing of crops, and took care of the livestock. In this context, the stereotypes of the good hunter, the brave warrior, and the forest statesman were the images of masculine success. However, between 1754, when the French and Indian War began, and the treaty at Big Tree in 1797, the Seneca sold their hunting grounds and became largely confined to eleven tiny isolated reservations. A series of economic, political, and military disasters made the maintenance of these ideals virtually impossible. The good hunter could no longer hunt, game was scarce, and it was dangerous to venture off reservation lands into areas controlled by hostile white men. Without arms and allies, the brave warrior could no longer fight and considered his family to be threatened by the growing military might of the United States. The forest statesman, the third ideal image, became an object of contempt.

For nearly a century, the Iroquois chiefs, including the Seneca tribe, had been able to play the British off the French, and the Americans off the British. From both they were able to obtain presents (guns, traps, axes, food, and drink) and promises of territorial integrity. As a necessity they maintained an extensive system of alliances among surrounding tribal groups. After the treaty, they were divested of their powers. The league of the Iroquois, of which they were a member, was no longer respected. Their political and economic alliances with western Native Americans broke down and they were regarded as cowards for having made peace with the white man.

The Seneca response to what was viewed as the destruction of their culture was pathological. Many became drunkards, witchcraft accusations increased, factionalism made common policy impossible, the household unit became unstable, brawling and fighting were common.

The initial stress was a deculturation stress as they witnessed their culture being destroyed. This led to the abuse of alcohol. Identifying the Indian as a drunkard became popular. As a result, federal laws were passed to prohibit the sale of alcohol on Indian reservations. Since Native Americans looked different, they weren't of the same "herd" as the white man. They couldn't fit in. This led to an acculturation stress when they attempted assimilation. These stresses persist to this day.

Chronic inescapable stress also occurs in the inner cities, in present-day Russia, in wartime combatants. Inescapable stress can come from many patterns. The patterns of poverty, hostility, fear, hopelessness, and uncertainty cause the brain to respond for its own survival. This process landscapes the brain.

The question remains, why do some people develop an addiction and not others? If the thread that ties all addicts together is their landscape, then those individuals whose terrains respond to stress by producing a *craving brain* will become addicts. Some individuals develop addictive behavior with little stress, others require enormous stress. There are some who will not develop it under any circumstances. Our hormones and our experiences can lower the serotonin level (and, as we shall see, dopamine levels) and make the nucleus accumbens more sensitive to patterns that elicit addictive behavior. It remains for us to explain the nature of addiction and why certain activities and substances are the focus of addictive behavior.

3

▼

THE CRAVING RESPONSE

Why is a glass of wine the prelude to a slide into oblivion for someone addicted to alcohol? Why does a bet for some become an unstoppable gamble? Why is a loaf of bread consumed without even making a sandwich? What converts a simple thought, sight, smell, or taste into an irresistible action?

"No one but another compulsive gambler can understand what I mean when I say that when I was gambling, there is nothing I wouldn't do." George Barton is a twice divorced fifty-six-year-old dry cleaner who owes over $250,000 to friends and bookies.

"From the time I was fifteen, when I started owing ten, twenty dollars I didn't have, I stopped sleeping through the night. Since those first bets, I knew I wasn't normal." The inescapable stress of being in debt had begun.

"For the last two years I've been gambling on sports. My week starts Monday and ends Sunday night. Every night after dinner I'd make a call and place my bets. I never needed cash because I didn't have to make good until the following week. It is the greatest feeling in the world. It's a high, a sense of relief, I can't explain. If for some reason the line was busy and the game would be starting in a few minutes, I'd go nuts. Dialing, dialing, and dialing. It's a horrible feeling, not being able to place a bet. Like mental agony."

We define addictive behavior as the *compulsive* use of a substance or activity. "Gotta have it" occurs because the brain produces a craving response for that substance or activity. No craving, no addictive behavior. No addictive behavior, no addiction.

What is craving? It is an uncomfortable, intrusive, obsessional response to a pattern that compels us to act to obtain the specific object or activity. Craving is an extreme biological response. Desire, want, and need are normal biological responses without the obsessional features that define craving. Originally, craving was a response that occurred only when survival was at stake. It occurred, for example, when a primal survival system had been activated for a prolonged time. The pain produced by this system was intense, allowing only those thoughts that would remove the pain. In a sense, the *craving response* is at one end of the spectrum of conditioned responses designed to motivate us to meet a need. Through our experience with needs and desires we know what it takes to extinguish the pain and give peace and contentment. We have learned it through a process called conditioned learning.

The pattern recognition and response to the sight of food transforms the hungry body. From a physiological point of view, the anticipation of the event—in this case, eating—becomes translated into the event itself. Salivation occurs, stomach acid increases, and the entire digestive apparatus is set in play. Dopamine rises in the nucleus accumbens to make us get the food. Ivan Pavlov, the great Russian scientist, called this an *unconditioned response*. In truth, it is a *conditioned response*. It is the first response that human infants learn. Conditioning begins at the mother's breast, where the taste and texture of this rich milk, called colostrum, causes salivation to aid the digestive process. Filled with enzymes to help break down this primal food, the salivary glands pump their juices into the mouth of the newborn. This is an unconditioned response. No training is needed here. The mother's milk on the baby's tongue directly stimulates the baby's salivary gland.

Pavlov found that salivation in response to the presentation of food could rapidly be transferred to another stimulus. In his classic experiments, Pavlov found that a bell tone repeatedly associated with the presentation of food (the first conditioned pattern) could, on its own, after a suitable number of trials, elicit the identical physiological reactions to the presentation of food. The animal associated the bell with sight of food and sight of food with food in the mouth. This association of food in the mouth with the bell produced the physiological response of salivation.

This type of learning fits into the natural life order. Nature wanted as many possible ways to motivate action that will stop the pain. Nature wanted the sight of an animal's footprints to be able to elicit a craving response. She wanted the scent of prey to make us act. When a specific need was brought to consciousness, she wanted us to respond physiologically and behaviorally to a variety of patterns in identical ways. She wanted to raise dopamine in the nucleus accumbens to motivate us to seek those things that can stop the pain. These are the conditioned responses that ensure survival. Once conditioned, and on the appropriate landscape, a pattern recognition process can produce an unstoppable response.

The critical questions then arise. What makes the response unstoppable? What directs it to alcohol, cocaine, caffeine, gambling, and narcotics? In essence, what produces addictive behavior? The answer lies in the ability of substances and activities to raise dopamine in the nucleus accumbens. Alcohol, cigarettes, cocaine, narcotics, and gambling do just that. This rise of dopamine then allows for the process of conditioned learning. As Pavlov showed (though not directly), this rise in dopamine can be transferred to other patterns. The jingle of ice cubes in a glass can raise dopamine if it has been associated with the ingestion of alcohol. It doesn't take the alcoholic long to recognize that where he sees a bar, he will find alcohol. This association conditionally raises dopamine and motivates behavior. He can't stop his feet from walking through the door (see below).

THE ROLE OF UNCONDITIONED STIMULI

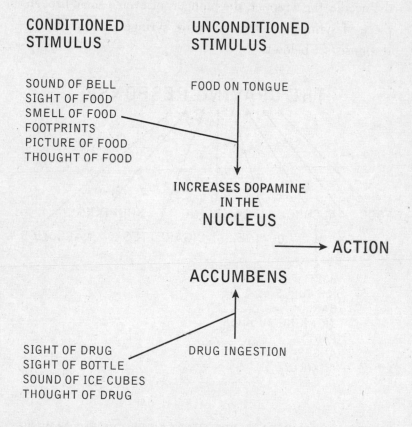

THE UNCONDITIONED STIMULUS SETS THE STAGE FOR ASSOCIATIVE LEARNING AND ACTION.

Each pattern recognition and response process must be conditioned separately. Seeing a junkie's syringe will not stimulate us to think narcotics if the needle has not been previously associated with the delivery of the drug. Once conditioned however, the ability to scan for connections allows just the needle, the wrapper, the plunger, or even a small broken piece of syringe to elicit the entire syringe and produce a response (see below).

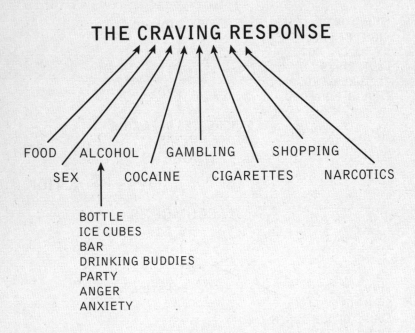

THE CRAVING RESPONSE

FOOD / ALCOHOL / GAMBLING / SHOPPING

SEX / COCAINE / CIGARETTES / NARCOTICS

BOTTLE
ICE CUBES
BAR
DRINKING BUDDIES
PARTY
ANGER
ANXIETY

THERE ARE MANY PATTERNS THAT CAN PRODUCE A CRAVING RESPONSE. ALL REQUIRE CONDITIONING, BUT ALL LEAD TO THE SAME CRAVING RESPONSE.

The survival systems that direct our behavior for food, sex, and safety create recognizable symptoms that make us act. They produce pain in the form of hunger, anxiety, and increased sexual desires. It is this stress that creates a craving landscape. So what system directs addictive behavior? There is none. Instead, it is the brain's landscapers, our hormones and the environment, that alter our inherent terrain and set the stage for a craving response. These forces produce a low-serotonin, sensitive nucleus accumbens landscape. This is the craving brain. There are no symptoms of hunger, no ache in the loins, no anxiety to tell us what to do. Nor can the craving brain tell itself that it's had enough. There is no regulator system to raise the serotonin and produce a sense of satiety. Instead, we respond to patterns that release dopamine in the nucleus accumbens. This explains why there is no common thread that ties all addicts together. The only thing they all share is a craving landscape. The craving response can therefore be directed to anything that unconditionally releases dopamine in the nucleus accumbens and anything that can be associated with the anticipation of obtaining that object or activity.

Several theories have tried to explain the origin of addictive behavior. The two we discuss here evoke the dual mechanisms for conditioning: pain and pleasure. Abraham Wikler, in his classic article on conditioning factors in addiction, proposes that the craving for alcohol or drugs represents the avoidance response to the pain of withdrawal. That is, the body experiences pain when the alcohol is leaving the body. While these symptoms may never reach consciousness (if, for example, only a small amount of alcohol was ingested), the subconscious brain remembers the experience and can produce a conditioned response that makes us act.

According to Wikler's theory, a small amount of alcohol should act like an hors d'oeuvre. That is, it should stimulate, not suppress, craving. Under the appropriate conditions, the effects of the first drink act as a stimulus that has been conditioned to an entire sequence of responses. Previous episodes have demonstrated that drinking can remove the subconscious pain associated with withdrawal. In other words, the first drink reminds us that if we continue drinking, we can take away the anticipated pain.

A rise in heart rate, tremulousness, and increased sweating are physiological responses to anxiety and nervousness. These reactions are also associated with the alcohol withdrawal syndrome. Wikler postulated that these symptoms, induced by arguments, loneliness, or fear, may likewise induce craving.

These researchers understood that while appropriate stimuli (e.g., beer glasses, a bar) represent the conditions necessary to evoke a conditioned withdrawal syndrome and hence produce craving and alcohol seeking, we cannot regard them as sufficient. They note that craving can also be highly influenced by mental set and physical setting. They believe that under ordinary circumstances the function of craving is to protect us against sensed danger, threat, or physical distress. By alerting us to a potential source of relief, we are encouraged to engage in efficient, goal-directed behavior.

A second theory, put forth by T. E. Robinson and K. C. Berridge, proposes that addictive drugs share the ability to enhance dopamine release in the nucleus accumbens. One function of the nucleus accumbens is to apply *incentive salience* to the way we perceive events. Incentive salience is a psychological process that transforms how we perceive stimuli by making them more attractive and wanted. These authors argue that repeated use of addictive drugs produces changes in the nucleus accumbens, rendering it increasingly and perhaps permanently sensitized to drugs. This sensitized nucleus accumbens is now conditioned to attribute increased importance to patterns associated with the act of drug taking. Thus, sensitization of the nucleus accumbens produces addictive behavior (compulsive drug seeking and drug taking) even if the expectation of drug pleasure is diminished, even in the face of punishment. This is particularly true of opiate addiction, where the addict insists that he is seeking the euphoric effect of the first dose and forgets the months or years of misery experienced during addiction. Ultimately, for these researchers, it is the drug that produces the problem.

While these two theories have much to commend them, they are incomplete. They provide a framework for the gotta-have-it part, but offer little information on the nature of the craving response, the role of environmental factors, what part our inherent dispositions play, what causes this behavior, or why we can't stop. To offer a more complete explanation of addictive behavior and the causes of the craving response, we must discuss the other roles that dopamine and serotonin play in the pattern recognition and response process. The information ahead is somewhat technical, but it is critical to unraveling what motivates addictive behavior.

NEUROMODULATORS

Neurotransmitters are chemicals that alter the frequency and intensity of the messages being sent. The greater the amount of neurotransmitters, the stronger the message. Dopamine and serotonin are not traditional neurotransmitters. Extensive evidence suggests that dopamine and serotonin may be acting both as neurotransmitters and *neuromodulators*. Neuromodulators act as filters, allowing more or less information to be processed. In their role as neuromodulators, we believe that dopamine and serotonin mediate the landscaping properties of our hormones and our environment. It is the levels of dopamine and serotonin outside the nucleus accumbens that influence our ability to convert sensation into perception and perception into a response.

Most neurons containing dopamine and serotonin are slow responders. Compared to other neurons, their baseline firing is low and stable. This results in a steady release of these substances. These neurons also exhibit a constricted range of firing, and they are unable to sustain high levels of activity. They behave as if it were important for dopamine and serotonin levels to be maintained within a set range, similar to our body's temperature regulating system. Each brain has its own unique baseline levels of dopamine and serotonin. It is these levels that modulate neural information processing.

Once dopamine and serotonin are released, their influences may last several seconds or even minutes, in contrast to the milliseconds following the release of classical neurotransmitters. The neurons that contain dopamine and serotonin do not make classical neuronal connections. Rather, they appear to be diffusely spread so that they can influence a wide area. Thus the release of dopamine and serotonin in this steady, often synchronous manner suggests that they interact to optimize the state of information processing.

Under stress, these levels are altered. If the stress is transient, the baseline levels of dopamine and serotonin are restored. If the stress is inescapable, the levels may be perpetually altered. As we shall see, the direction and magnitude of these changes are adaptations that are made by the brain designed to increase the chances of survival.

DOPAMINE

How does dopamine act to influence the state of pattern recognition processing? It appears that dopamine modulates the responsiveness of cells. A landscape that is high in dopamine makes more connections with perceived patterns than a landscape with low dopamine. This improves the odds that when we perceive a pattern it will lead to a desired response. Dopamine not only enhances response to the desired pattern, it decreases the response to backfield information. This phenomenon is analogous to the effect of contrast enhancement on photocopy machines. When the machine transforms gray areas into either black or white, things stand out. The subtleties are lost, however, and some valuable information is not utilized. But in terms of a survival advantage, this is exactly what we want. We do not want to be distracted by nonessential patterns. We want to remain focused on the objects that are being directed by the primal survival system.

High levels of dopamine are reflected in sharper thinking and focused behavior. It has long been established that substances that raise dopamine levels, like amphetamines, improve our signal detection and accuracy. During the Second World War, radar operators given amphetamines exhibited improved concentration and a dramatic reduction in errors. Dopamine, in essence, makes the sensing of things we need to know about clearer.

This improved signal detection requires that dopamine be present in the brain. Cortical (higher-functioning) neurons appear to operate at high gain (lots of dopamine) during periods of wakefulness and *arousal*. At the end of a stimulating and stressful day, we have used up most of our brain dopamine, leaving us feeling exhausted. We sleep to allow the brain to restore the dopamine during periods of low arousal and low dopamine utilization. The levels of dopamine also appear to have effects on how we feel. Low levels of dopamine are associated with depression, fuzzy thinking, and the inability to block out extraneous signals. This is why our ability to concentrate decreases as the day goes on and why, after a good sleep, everything looks brighter in the morning when dopamine is restored. Overall, the neuromodulating function of dopamine is to increase the state of arousal, hence making the processing of sensory input quicker and sharper. Dopamine also lowers the threshold for making connections and provides the mechanism for prioritizing input. Spotting your child's wisp of hair in a crowd requires a high level of dopamine.

As discussed in previous chapters, dopamine acts as a neurotransmitter and motivates action when it is released in the nucleus accumbens. Patterns that activate this local release of dopamine provide the activation message: Gotta have it! In addition to its neural information and neurotransmitter role, dopamine also drives the motor system. The motor system and the nucleus accumbens are side-by-side in the brain. It makes sense that when we perceive something we need, the body moves to get it. Both are driven by dopamine.

SEROTONIN

If dopamine facilitates information flow, the modulatory action of serotonin is to constrain it. Serotonin reduces the ability to make connections. High serotonin states make memory retrieval difficult. A greater number of associations must be made to bring the desired information to consciousness. These are the properties of dopamine and serotonin that are balanced by the brain and modified depending on the circumstances. If we need to increase an object's importance, dopamine rises. If we want to diminish its importance, serotonin needs to be increased. When we are under chronic inescapable stress, serotonin levels drop and allow a less constrained dopamine to search for a way out of our troubles.

Thus the neural information processing system balances dopamine, which increases connections and focus, and serotonin, which constrains sensory input so that too much information is not brought to the forefield. The modulatory action of serotonin in information processing systems may be viewed as one of constraint, because the role of neuromodulation is not to suppress information but rather to regulate the threshold to activation. Serotonin's role as a modulator of information can be conceptualized as (a) preventing overshoot of other dynamic elements and (b) controlling the amount of information that is processed.

The need to prevent overshoot is the need for satiety, for a sense of completion, a finishing of the task. Think about the possibility of having no way to stop an action once it starts. Removing serotonin from the brain of a rat causes compulsive sexual activity and insatiable eating. Dopamine no longer has serotonin to balance it. The animal will continue to have sex and eat even if a warning *cue* to a shock is given or even the shock itself. Punishment does not appear to deter a low-serotonin brain when it is driven by dopamine. This is what drives the unstoppable craving.

The other role of serotonin is to control the amount of information that is processed. Sensory input from the field must be modulated so that sensory overload doesn't occur. Dopamine and serotonin are complementary in being able to inhibit or stimulate data. When we consciously focus on one sense, we decrease our ability to use other senses. Thus when we are consciously focusing our eyes on an object (bringing it into the forefield), our hearing and other sensory organs experience a diminution of activity. The brain does this subconsciously. If we are concentrating on reading, for example, our auditory threshold is raised. If someone wants to get our attention, he or she has to speak louder. We can accomplish this on the conscious level as well. When we really want to smell something, we close our eyes, decreasing forefield sensory input (no forefield objects to raise dopamine) to the visual system. This enhances our ability to discriminate odors. We will shut off the car radio when we are lost and trying to find a familiar landmark. Without this ability, the brain would become sensory overloaded and any processing would be impossible. Even with this brilliant system, the brain can sometimes give us a busy signal.

Social behavior also appears to be affected by serotonin. In primates, serotonin facilitates social behavior. Those patterns that elicit anxiety and fear are diminished with high levels of serotonin. There is a decrease in avoidance behavior and social solitude. It is what holds herds together. Decreases in serotonin may alter the response of the animal to signals that normally constrain social behavior. Abnormally low levels of serotonin may result in inappropriate anger, aggressiveness, and impulsivity.

The neurotransmitter function of serotonin is also critical. It comes into play when there is an acute need to control input. Our brain will protect us by involuntarily raising serotonin when we experience a life-threatening situation. Very high serotonin levels can make us nauseated and cause vomiting. This explains why we vomit when we see something horrible. There is an involuntary rise in brain serotonin designed to decrease the impact of what we have just seen. We see things in slow motion as serotonin constrains our processing. The brain involuntarily decreases our ability to register new incoming data as a way of protecting us from the pain that might occur. This is also why some people freeze in life-threatening situations. Serotonin inhibits dopamine's locomotor activity. We often have little recall of these traumatic events. It is a traumatic amnesia, driven by serotonin.

To summarize, dopamine and serotonin function to modulate the type and quantity of information that is processed. They affect our responses to patterns. They affect mood and social behavior. For brief times, they also motivate us and bring us peace.

THE CRAVING RESPONSE

The desire for food is driven by forefield symptoms of hunger. These symptoms act as a recognizable pattern that motivates us to get something to eat. The primal survival system brings these symptoms to consciousness. This forefield pattern recognition can be either acted upon or ignored, at least in the short run. Other times, a backfield pattern recognition process can make us get something to eat. Say we're walking down the street, not thinking about much, enjoying the day, and we smell popcorn. Involuntarily, if our landscape and our nucleus accumbens is sensitive, we will salivate and more than likely go get that popcorn. This is part of the backfield pattern recognition leading to a behavioral response process. The subconscious smell produced two responses: First, it made us aware of the popcorn; then it motivated us to get some. If we were walking down the street with popcorn on our minds (in our forefield), our ability to prioritize our attention would have allowed us to visually pick up the popcorn stand in the distance. We would have also become aware of the popcorn aroma sooner. Indeed, if for some reason we were craving popcorn, our approach would have been even more directed.

The primal responses for food, sex, and safety are driven by the same system. Under normal circumstances, the pain that drives us is minimal and the pleasure obtained by completing the task is great. However, when a craving response is produced, we are motivated by the desire to relieve the pain.

As mentioned previously, the craving response has two components, the "gotta have it" and "I got it."

To create the "gotta have it," any one of the three survival systems must cause distress. Hunger, fear, and unconsummated sexual desires are stressful. Through the symptoms they produce, the survival systems promote thoughts of food, sex, or anxiety and raise dopamine in the brain to allow us to better identify patterns that would lead to the removal of the discomfort. Each also increases the sensitivity of the nucleus accumbens to patterns that release dopamine. The serotonin is lowered to increase the likelihood of making a connection and bringing it to consciousness. A craving response for food, sex and safety, then, is rising dopamine on a landscape of low serotonin. The individual is highly motivated and aroused. After we respond and have completed the activity, the survival system feeds back information to the brain and serotonin levels are raised ("got it"). The processing of information is constrained. Patterns no longer stimulate the rise in dopamine in the nucleus accumbens. "Getting it" leads to a high-serotonin, high-dopamine state. The brain is biobalanced for that particular substance or activity. This stops the pain. For a time, we are content and can choose not to be motivated to action.

Unlike the three survival systems, a craving brain that is produced by our genetics, hormones, and environment does not generate symptoms that drive behavior. All that drives the behavior is the craving response, the rise of dopamine in the nucleus accumbens caused by substances or activities on a low-serotonin landscape. There is no awareness of pain except the pain of craving. There is no pain relief when action is taken. Getting it is all that matters. If we crave alcohol, for example, responding to and getting alcohol affects only this specific craving. Since there is no sensing system in place, getting it does not produce a rise in serotonin. The "got it" never happens. With the serotonin already low, the dopamine is unconstrained, and the "gotta have it" becomes unstoppable. Overshoot takes place. The conditioned rise of dopamine just keeps on going until either we run out of dopamine or another process intervenes.

What about addictive behavior involving food or sex? It would seem that the survival system would be able to prevent this from occurring because eating or having sex should stop the behavior. Despite what we observe, the compulsive desire to eat or have sex is not driven by hunger or sexual desires, but by a pattern recognition process. Under these conditions, food or sex cannot alter the craving brain. If the action is driven by pattern recognition and the activity does not, in and of itself, raise serotonin, the craving brain will remain.

Interestingly, there are substances that do raise both dopamine and serotonin. Nicotine and heroin can do this for short periods of time and the behavior will stop. This reflects the ability of these substances to alter the neural information processing. This is why we reach for a cigarette when the dopamine goes off in our brain. After experiencing anxiety from the boss's phone call, cigarettes raise serotonin and calm the brain. Since, unfortunately, nothing happened to change the conditions that landscaped the craving brain, it returns as soon as these substances are out of the body. Nicotine produces only short-lived changes in the brain so that repeated intake is necessary. This explains the phenomenon of chain-smoking in someone who has a craving brain.

The inability to biobalance the landscape by completing the craving response allows for other processes to be conditioned. This leads to the development of addictive behavior that can be directed to multiple substances and activities. This is the addictive personality. An ex-drinker might gamble and use cocaine. An ex–compulsive shopper may exercise incessantly. Or they may do all concurrently.

HIGH-DOPAMINE AND LOW-DOPAMINE CRAVING BRAINS

As we said, chronic inescapable stress increases the sensitivity of the nucleus accumbens and lowers serotonin. If the patterns and thought processes produce a sense of hopelessness, then this pattern recognition lowers dopamine as well. This is designed for survival purposes. A lowered dopamine level decreases both the pattern recognition of harshness and the connections that bring these images to conscious awareness, lowering our distress. In contrast, if the stress is anxiety provoking, dopamine will be elevated, making us more vigilant.

The body adapts to maximize survival. A chronically

stressful environment can either raise or lower dopamine. It will always lower serotonin. In both cases, the nucleus accumbens is sensitized. Thus a craving brain can be a low-dopamine or a high-dopamine state, and this will be reflected in the behavior of these individuals. An individual with a low-dopamine, low-serotonin landscape has a harder time learning. Setting and keeping long-term goals that require delayed gratification is extremely difficult. This landscape ignites impulsive behavior, awakens the need to herd, and can produce depression. Someone in a high-dopamine, low-serotonin state tends to be brighter, more vigilant, aggressive, and can juggle many things at the same time. This person might behave impulsively, have extramarital affairs, tend to carry about thirty extra pounds, and exhibit false confidence. And then there are the millions of types of craving brains in between.

WHAT WE CRAVE

What makes us crave different things? In countries like France, where wine consumption is high and socially accepted, addictive behavior with regard to alcohol is high as well. In some of our inner cities, the availability of crack cocaine coupled with so few cultural sanctions against its use is associated with the increased rates of addiction to crack. It is less common to find accompanying psychological disorders among people who abuse socially acceptable substances or activities, such as food or exercise. This contrasts with the significant psychological problems that arise when there are serious restrictions on the use of the abused substance. Craving brains can be mild, moderate, or severe. It appears that social restrictions can control choice, if the serotonin is not too low. The stress caused by breaking cultural taboos appears to affect the use and abuse of many activities. However, if our landscapes are severely primed for craving, no social constraints will stop us.

Although widespread availability and cultural mores are risk factors for use, addictive disorders tend to develop in the context of individual risk factors. Our inherent terrain, the onset of puberty, and certainly our environment determine the intensity our addictive behavior will take.

"If you grew up on the Lower East Side of New York during the 1950s and didn't gamble, that was unusual," George Barton remembers, discussing the roots of his forty-four years as a gambler. "When I was seven, my father started taking me with him to the Democratic Club. He played cards there two, three nights a week after dinner. I'd stand behind his chair for hours, fascinated by the logic and excited by the real chance of winning. In the summer, we'd take the bus to Trotters. By the time I was twelve, I was betting with money I earned delivering chickens.

"Gambling was entertainment. Saturday night, my parents had a regular card game with their friends. When we were younger, we would play a card game called bundles, outside on the stoop. As we got older, we'd walk to the pool hall. I didn't have the skill to play, but I'd bet on a friend or go upstairs where they had a ticker tape machine with the results of all the games and races. There'd be three or four bookmakers who'd hang out there, taking any bet you'd want to make.

"As a teenager, you played to belong. If you folded, you weren't in the action with the other guys. You weren't in the group. I remember using my high school physics textbook to figure out how to adjust for the wind at the track. My dad loved that."

George's early experiences in an environment that produced chronic inescapable stress created George Barton, the compulsive gambler.

If left untreated, the craving response produced by a pattern recognition process on a craving landscape is often progressive and even fatal. Characterized by a loss of control over a particular substance or activity, it can be initiated by patterns that occur in either the forefield or the backfield. All of the activities to which addicts turn are driven by the craving response that raises dopamine in the nucleus accumbens on a landscape of low serotonin. We reiterate, the survival system produces the most powerful force in nature. It is the drive to survive. How do we go about solving this biologically driven problem?

4

▼

BATTLING FOR CONTROL

The battle to control the craving response is waged one day at a time, one hour at a time, even one minute at a time. It pits our minds against a most formidable enemy, our brains. The victor wins control over our behavior. This is an old fight that has engaged millions of soldiers in a never-ending internal struggle. Scientists, physicians, theologians, and psychologists are all involved in the search for a resolution. The quest continues. There seems to be no single answer, but many different ones, with each individual seeking a path that works the best. What have we learned so far? What can those who have struggled and succeeded teach us?

A way to prevent the craving response was discovered

2,500 years ago by one of the greatest thinkers of all time, Siddhartha Gautama, a sixth-century–B.C. prince of India. At the age of twenty-nine, this young man who wanted for nothing left his wife and family to set off on a series of wanderings, seeking the cause and solution to the problem of suffering. Six years later, through meditation, he discovered the cause and found a solution. The origin of suffering was craving, and the solution was to follow the Eightfold Path.

Basic to Buddha's teaching was the theme of liberation, freeing oneself from selfish desires, self-centered malice, and despair. For Buddha, this was a claim of no small significance, for it meant liberation from one's own *samskaras*—the conditioned mental attitudes and responses. Buddha had found a way to prevent the conditioned craving response. He became the personification of the unconditioned mind. This liberation from suffering and reinstitution of human freedom can happen only through detachment, being free of desire. How did he accomplish this? The Buddha said:

> And I discovered that profound truth, so difficult to perceive, difficult to understand, tranquilizing and sublime, which is not to be gained by mere reasoning, and is visible only to the wise. That liberation only occurs when we are free of suffering. What now is the Noble Truth of Suffering? Birth is suffering; decay is suffering; death is suffering; sorrow, lamentation, pain, grief and despair are suffering; not to get what

one desires is suffering; in short, the five groups of existence are suffering.

Buddha understood that life was filled with inescapable stress.

What, now, is the Noble Truth of the Origin of Suffering? It is craving which gives rise to fresh rebirth, and, bound up with pleasure and lust, now here, now there, finds ever-fresh delight. But where there are delightful and pleasurable things, there this craving rises and takes root. Eye, ear, nose, tongue, body and mind are delightful and pleasurable: there this craving arises and takes root.

Buddha understood that our senses were the sources of craving.

What, now, is the Noble Truth of the Extinction of Suffering? It is the complete fading away and extinction of this craving, its forsaking and abandonment, liberation and detachment from it. The extinction of greed, the extinction of hate, the extinction of delusion, this indeed is called *Nirvana*.

Buddha understood that without removing the cravings there would be no peace.

For the Buddhist, "salvation" means extinction of suffering, release from the wearisome cycle of birth and rebirth. This Nirvana is attained through following the Eightfold Path: right understanding, right intentions, right speech, right conduct, right means of livelihood, right endeavor, right mindfulness, and right contemplation. Following this path requires mental discipline, moral conduct, and the wisdom to see things as they are. For Buddha, the jingle of ice cubes would never have produced a craving for alcohol. Ice cubes are ice cubes.

While we cannot hope to exclude all the external objects, words, and sounds that impinge on our senses and give rise to passions, we can, through Buddha's Eightfold Path, control the mind so that it will not mistake unpleasant, impure, and impermanent things as desirable. After rigorous training, the individual is not only able to control his mind but, when needed, empty it of all contents so that the mind remains serene.

Buddha taught that none of our attachments, whether they be pleasures and possessions or convictions and beliefs, are eternal and permanent. If we cling to any one and believe it is an end in itself, it will lead us to craving, which will lead us to suffering. Since, he explains, we are each made up of a constantly changing combination of matter, sensation, perception, predisposition, and consciousness, we have no permanent self or soul. At any given moment, we are the temporary sum total of our sensory awareness.

Once we realize that the self is only an ever-changing

stream of ephemeral processes, we can lose our attachments to the permanent world. By steadfastly adhering to the Eightfold Path, we can achieve Nirvana and extinguish the flames of passion. Only when we have achieved this state does suffering end.

THE DISCOVERY OF ADDICTION

In order to formulate a plan to treat addictive behavior, we must first understand what causes it. While Buddha believed that the senses caused the craving, modern thought began by utilizing a disease model so that treatment could be directed toward ending the craving response.

The theory that addictive behavior, alcoholism specifically, is a progressive disease is about two hundred years old. Its chief symptom is loss of control over the use of the substance; its only remedy is abstinence. Before this time, it was assumed people drank because they wanted to, not because they couldn't stop themselves.

"Thus, when a drunkard has his liquor before him, and he has to choose whether to drink or not . . . If he wills to drink, then drinking is the proper object of his will; and drinking, on some account or other, now appears most agreeable to him and suits him best. If he chooses to refrain, then refraining is the immediate object of his will and is most pleasing to him." So said Jonathan Edwards in his analysis of drunkenness published in 1754.

It is easy to understand this position. There were times when an alcoholic could resist and remain sober and other times when he found drinking irresistible. The decision not to drink, while probably a rare event for alcoholics, reinforced the concept of choice. Drunkenness was viewed as a weakness of will. If a man can say no once, he can say no twice. If twice, then three times, and so on. The drunk makes a choice for pleasure, for sobriety could be willed.

In 1810 Dr. Benjamin Rush published what was to become the outline of the modern conception of alcohol addiction. According to Rush, drunkards were "addicted" to alcohol. He describes the progressive nature of the disease as episodic drinking with progressively shorter and shorter intervals between drinking bouts. As for the loss of control, he anecdotally remarks that, "When strongly urged by one of his friends, to leave off drinking (an habitual drunkard) said 'Were a keg of rum in one corner of the room, and were a cannon constantly discharging balls between me and it, I could not refrain from passing before that cannon, in order to get the rum.'" If one wished not to drink, Dr. Rush advised, "Taste not, handle not and touch not."

Using Rush's insights, the temperance movement, firmly committed to the necessity for total abstinence, began, and by 1830, over a half million Americans swore off alcohol. In 1838 S. B. Woodward, the then leading American physician concerned with mental health, described alcohol addiction this way: "The appetite is wholly physical, depending on a condition of the stomach and the nervous system, which transcends all ordinary motives of abstinence. The suffering is immense, and the desire of immediate relief so entirely uncontrollable, that it is quite questionable whether the moral power of many of its victims is sufficient to withstand its imperative demands."

Woodward agreed that abstention was the only cure. Because liquor was readily available and thought to be addicting, the drunk was viewed as a victim of alcohol's power. By the latter part of the nineteenth century, groups like the 300,000-member Sons of Temperance provided addicts who joined their organization with encouragement, friendship, and a social life free of alcohol.

Prohibition followed the temperance movement. The drunkard was no longer seen as a poor, helpless victim of the addictive properties of alcohol. Now he was becoming a pest and a menace. Under prohibition, an alcoholic was now viewed as a criminal, someone who broke the laws of the land. This view remains intact with regard to the currently illegal drugs.

The rediscovery of alcoholism as a disease that affected only certain individuals was a significant shift. In the 1960s E. M. Jellinik wrote the defining work on the disease concept of alcoholism. His main thesis was that people who were unable to abstain suffered from alcoholism. Alcoholism became scientifically accepted as a person-specific addiction. In Jellinik's terms, there was a loss of control. From such a definition of behavior beyond the control of the will stems the solution.

THE FELLOWSHIP OF ALCOHOLICS ANONYMOUS

June 10, 1935, was the first day of permanent sobriety for Doctor Bob and the birth of an organization called Alcoholics Anonymous. It began as a fellowship for those who had hit bottom and offered the reward of support, friendship, and an alcohol-free social structure as a positive substitute for the destructive call of alcohol.

Its fundamental principles are described in the first edition of *The Big Book,* which declares that "We are more than one hundred men and women who have recovered from a seemingly hopeless state of body and mind." The method used is summarized in the twelve steps of Alcoholics Anonymous. For alcoholics and those trapped in other addictive behaviors like gambling, narcotics, sex, eating, and smoking, the AA program of twelve steps provides a plan to help gain control. As *The Big Book* explains, alcoholism is "cunning, baffling, and powerful," and constant vigilance is required to combat it. There is no easy or soft way. Total commitment is required.

Attendance at ninety meetings in ninety days is strongly encouraged to begin. This comes after the most important step, admitting that one is an alcoholic and powerless over alcohol. Only then can a person take those steps that will free him or her from the craving. Those steps require removing the cloak of *denial* and exposing one's pain. In addition, the program requires daily meditation and prayer, the reading of AA literature, especially *The Big Book*, and the application of the twelve-step principles to everyday affairs.

The twelve-step plan of action is carefully described in the basic text of *The Big Book*. It states:

1. We admitted we are powerless over alcohol, and that our lives have become unmanageable.

2. Came to believe that a Power greater than ourselves could restore us to sanity.

3. Made a decision to turn our will and our lives over to the care of God as we understood Him.

4. Made a searching and fearless moral inventory of ourselves.

5. Admitted to God, to ourselves, and to another human being the exact nature of our wrongs.

6. Were entirely ready to have God remove all these defects of character.

7. Humbly ask Him to remove our shortcomings.

8. Made a list of all the people we had harmed, and became willing to make amends to them all.

9. Made direct amends to such people wherever possible, except when to do so would injure them or others.

10. Continued to take a personal inventory and when we were wrong promptly admitted it.

11. Sought through prayer and meditation to improve our conscious contact with God as we understood Him, praying only for knowledge of His will for us and the power to carry that out.

12. Having had a spiritual awakening as the result of these steps, we tried to carry this message to alcoholics and to practice these principles in all our affairs.*

At AA meetings everywhere, in schools and churches, prisons and hospitals, the "drunk," protected by anonymity, admits his alcoholism before the group. On the walls are often framed, hand-scripted slogans: first things first; think, think, think; one day at a time. Acknowledgment that alcoholism is a disease for which abstinence is the only answer follows. Most

---

*The Twelve Steps are reprinted with permission of Alcoholics Anonymous World Services Inc. Permission to reprint the Twelve Steps does not mean that AA has approved the contents of this publication or that AA agrees with the views expressed herein. AA is a program of recovery from alcoholism *only*—use of the Twelve Steps in connection with programs and activities that are patterned after AA but address other problems, or in any other non-AA context, does not imply other- wise.

members believe they will never be rid of their addiction, but instead will always be "in recovery." Although many feel that their lives have been saved by AA, they cannot explain exactly how or why it works. But they do believe they stay sober by helping others stay sober too.

Ann Malone is a thirty-seven-year-old commercial artist recently celebrating three years free of drugs, alcohol, and overeating. After twenty-three years of addictive behavior, she credits AA with turning her life around. "AA is the best thing that ever happened to me. I think that for a lot of addicts and alcoholics, one of the key things that happens to them is they withdraw from the human race, when, in fact, it's an irony, what they need most is other people. This is the first place that I ever felt that I belonged, that people cared about me. My first year was a constant battle. I was a big snob. I was grandiose. I have a successful career, and I'm sitting in the same room with all these drunks. And meanwhile, I've grown to love and respect all these people, regardless of where they came from or what they do today. It's a tremendous support system. It's magic and nobody can really put their finger on why it works. None of the scientists, nobody.

"We all understand each other. When anybody says any-thing—positive, negative, good experience, bad experience—we all connect, and it's on a spiritual level. The experience and situations are so different from person to person. It's the feelings and the way of thinking that are so common. It's the negative side of our personalities that tend to want to come out and take over and destroy anything positive that we're doing for ourselves. It's that evil demon that we call the disease of alcoholism. I felt so connected, yet for the longest time I had the hardest time trusting and believing that they really did care about me. That's why one of the common slogans of AA is: 'Keep coming back. We'll love you until you learn to love yourself.' I would never have met these people and chosen to be friends with them in any other situation.

"My first year, a whole bunch of people threw me a party for my anniversary. People send cards. They remember your name. They ask about you. You know, that's partly because this world has become a very lonely place and alcoholics all have in common the fact that they isolate. When I go into an AA room, I feel a part of it. I feel safe. I keep going back to 'spiritual'—because it's not something you can even put into words. AA is my bridge back to life."

THE MINNESOTA MODEL

The Minnesota Model, developed over thirty years ago, has its roots in the temperance movement. It is today's version of Dr. Rush's "sober house," a place where addicts could get special treatment "until the disease or morbid appetite are effectually removed." Treatment commonly starts with a twenty-eight-day inpatient stay to begin the process of rehabilitation. Viewing alcoholism as an incurable disease, it involves group counseling to confront the "denying" drunk, education about alcohol's consequences, and the confessional self-help AA protocol. Lay therapists who are themselves "in recovery" from alcoholism or drug dependence are an integral part of the comprehensive, multiprofessional approach.

Ex-addict leaders run group therapy sessions sharing life histories, providing written assignments, and encouraging peer evaluation. The sessions involve those families of the alcoholics and drug abusers who are willing to help support their patients. In an environment isolated from the subculture of alcohol and drugs and immersed in the spiritualism and support of AA, many patients report not simply abstinence from mood-altering chemicals, but an almost religious conversion.

Whether the tack is confrontational like Synanon, military in-your-face like Phoenix House, or gentler like the highly regarded Hazeldon Foundation in Center City, Minnesota, patients are encouraged to continue with some type of aftercare program for at least a year. This might include AA, individual or group therapy, or a center-sponsored program that continues the same type of activities offered during the intensive inpatient treatment.

For those who find the religious atmosphere of AA unappealing, there is Rational Recovery. Based on the philosophy of psychologist Albert Ellis, the ten-year-old program believes that psychological difficulties are caused by irrational beliefs that can be overcome through rational self-examination rather than religious belief. Unlike AA, Rational Recovery accepts members who still drink, demands only a once or twice a week commitment, and expects that after six months to a year, members are well enough to go on without them.

LOOKING FOR A SOBRIETY PILL

Historically, drug treatment for addictions has been the least successful and least available alternative. In 1948 Antabuse (disulfiram) was introduced. If you drink while taking the drug, nausea, vomiting, anxiety, and palpitations develop within minutes.

Conditioned aversion methods, associating an unpleasant experience with drug taking, has not met with great enthusiasm. Often the drinker will stop taking it because the physiological effects are so devastating, death is feared.

In 1965 Vincent Dole, an endocrinologist, and Marie Nyswander, a psychiatrist, reported addicts taking oral methadone experienced neither withdrawal symptoms nor euphoria from the new drug. They theorized that long-term heroin use resulted in a permanent metabolic imbalance requiring daily medication, much like diabetes.

Methadone maintenance is based on the hypothesis that, as a result of the repeated use of opioids, the addict sustains a metabolic alteration. For months and years after withdrawal, he experiences a feeling of abnormality (opioid hunger) that can only be relieved by opioids. By providing the opioid—methadone—under controlled conditions, many patients report little or no craving for opioids. This is in contrast to alcohol, where instead of suppressing cravings, the first drink often leads to further drinking.

When supplied with the dim echo of heroin (described as the difference between sipping wine all day versus gulping a shot of whiskey), many were able to resume relatively normal lives. Of course, many more found that the feeling of reassurance methadone supplied was no match for heroin's rush. Even when methadone is successful in controlling craving for narcotics, the abuse of other substances, such as alcohol, cocaine, and nicotine, remains a problem.

Researchers learned twenty years ago that use of the opioid blocker *naltrexone* could rob heroin and morphine of their power to intoxicate us by covering the receptors they attach to in the nervous system. Recently, it was discovered to be effective with alcohol as well. By reducing the euphoria of alcohol and dampening the craving for another drink, it helps patients feel better and encourages them to remain abstinent.

Along with fighting the battle against the craving response, many addicts also face depression and anxiety and exhibit antisocial behavior. Psychotherapy, antidepressants, and antianxiety drugs are often helpful in alleviating these symptoms. Dealing with these behaviors as part of a comprehensive treatment program is critical in helping addicts remain sober.

The details of how biology and psychology interact to create these relentless, tenacious behaviors is still a mystery.

Spiritual enlightenment, psychological insights, and pharmacological supports are helpful, but only for some and not always permanently. Nothing offers a cure. The primitive systems designed to ensure our survival have been forced to serve an additional master. These forces can overpower every attempt made to control them. What we need is a new battle plan, a different way of looking at battling the craving response.

5

▼

BIOBALANCE

The craving response is the force behind the drive to survive. It is the involuntary behavioral response we employ when our lives are at stake. Why are some of the approaches we've mentioned earlier sometimes successful in battling these powerful commands? Can we understand their success in terms of the biology of the brain? Will this understanding lead us to a new approach to treating addictive behavior?

As we said before, the earliest recorded method to stop craving was developed by Siddhartha, the founder of Buddhism. Siddhartha understood very well the impossible task of preventing pattern recognition from inflaming the passions and producing a craving response. It is even possible that Siddhartha himself suffered from a craving brain. He tried the road of abstinence, he tried the road of excess, neither worked. What he ultimately found was that by following the Eightfold Path, he could avoid the conditioned responses of the brain that led to craving.

How can we avoid forefield pattern recognition such as the jingling of ice cubes in a glass? Can we hope to avoid backfield pattern recognition even though no specific pattern can be discerned when we just walk through a neighborhood where we once practiced the addictive behavior? Each of these can elicit a powerful craving response. Because small parts of a pattern can be perceived as a whole pattern, there are an infinite number of patterns or pieces of patterns that can stimulate the craving response.

Buddha's clever solution was not to fight the craving response once it occurred, but instead to prevent the pattern recognition process before it began. He explained that we had to fill our minds with the right thoughts, do the right things, and act the right way so that nothing that might possibly stimulate the brain's craving response can enter the forefield or the backfield. This is no small task. Buddha said that if you wanted to have a smooth journey in life, all the roads you travel should be covered with leather. That way no matter where you would go, the road would be smooth. But Buddha understood that there was not enough leather to cover all the roads. He suggested that instead we wear leather shoes, so that regardless of where our foot might step, there would always be leather underneath. Buddha is saying that if our minds are filled with only the right things, then the wrong things that stimulate the passions, even if they are in the backfield, will be unable to produce a craving response. This concept is similar to the focusing of our senses where our thresholds to respond to nonforefield stimuli are increased. This reduction in forefield responsiveness probably occurs for backfield as well.

We hear stories all the time that addictive behavior began when a person was bored or unstimulated. If being "right" is our focus, other pattern recognition processes will be inhibited. Keeping our field focused on "right" things can avoid a perception that can lead to a craving response. Ultimately, these conditioned responses are extinguished.

Buddha also understood that if a pattern recognition process was initiated, it was important for us to have the ability to empty our minds of everything. Here he suggests meditation, which results in a conditioned rise in serotonin and a constraint of neural transmissions. The high serotonin level would prevent matches, leaving the mind empty. The pattern recognition process would be unable to lead to a craving response. As we mentioned previously, Buddha's teaching, which prevents and extinguishes conditioned learning, made him the perfect example of an unconditioned man.

Buddha's view that we are all ephemeral creatures is also liberating. Our goal in life should be the complete understanding that: "All formations are transient; all formations are subject to suffering; all things are without a self. Therefore, whatever there be of form, of feeling, perception, mental formations, or consciousness, whether past or present or future, one's own or external, gross or subtle, lofty or low, far or near, one should understand according to reality and true wisdom; this does not belong to me; this I am not; this is not my Self." If there are no attachments, there can be no loss. No loss, no suffering. No suffering, no inescapable stress.

NATURE SOLVES THE PROBLEM

Is the only way to stop the drive to survive to fill the mind with the "right" way? It is extraordinarily difficult for an individual to achieve this selfless discipline perfected by Buddha. Fortunately, Nature herself provides another solution. Her answer lies in how she stops the survival craving response.

To recapitulate, when any one of the primal survival systems is activated, the stress that our hunger, fear, or sexual desires produces causes an increase in the sensitivity of the nucleus accumbens. We are motivated to action when the nucleus accumbens releases dopamine as a conditioned response to the perception of the desired object or any perception that has been associated with the desired object. If, as in periods of starvation, this survival system has been activated for a prolonged time, a time-dependent decrease in serotonin is also produced. This adaptive process is useful for survival processes. The low serotonin allows dopamine to permit lots of matches. The sensitive nucleus accumbens reacts to release dopamine at the slightest hint of a match. With lowered serotonin, the brain's landscape exhibits the potential for overshoot. This leads to an exaggerated response to the pattern, the unconstrained action of dopamine, the now familiar "gotta have it" that is craving. The match can come from a thought, a sight, a smell, a taste, or a touch of an object. It can be in the forefield or the backfield. It need only have the slightest resemblance to the conditioning stimulus to evoke a craving response.

When the motivated task is completed, the primal survival system, sensing the need has been met, sends the message that no more has to be done. The level of serotonin goes up. The pain disappears, and the survival system has produced a biobalanced state for that specific pattern. We say we're in a biobalanced state when the pattern recognition process can no longer motivate behavior. Neural information processing for those patterns can no longer raise dopamine in the nucleus accumbens.

If Pavlov's hungry dog, conditioned to salivate at the sound of a bell, was fed just before the bell was rung, would he still salivate? The answer is no. A biobalanced state after eating reflects the high levels of dopamine and serotonin. The bright clearness of high dopamine, coupled with the ability of high serotonin to decrease *salience*, produces a contented state. The sight of food no longer produces a physiological response.

How can we stop a craving response once it has been initiated? If we have a craving landscape, made so by *genetics*, hormones, or inescapable stress, the thought of alcohol or any other substance or compulsive activity raises dopamine both in the nucleus accumbens to activate behavior and elsewhere in the brain. To biobalance the brain under these conditions, we need to raise scrotonin.

Being a member of Alcoholics Anonymous accomplishes this. When a pattern stimulates the craving for alcohol on a craving brain, the nucleus accumbens releases dopamine. Those who have "worked" the program can produce a conditioned response to this craving. AA uses the primal survival system for safety as the way to raise serotonin. It is through the feelings of fellowship (herd) and safety (which is why it is anonymous) that this is accomplished. We learn to raise serotonin in response to patterns and perceptions that promote our sense of belonging. Our ability to accomplish this is derived from nature's need to make us herd. Alcoholics Anonymous transfers the rise in serotonin from the herd to the fellowship. That's why attendance is strongly suggested for the first ninety days. This earns you entrance into the fellowship. Later, giving back to sponsor another member will bring an even greater sense of belonging. The fellowship engendered in all the twelve-step programs—Alcoholics, Overeaters, Gamblers, and Narcotics Anonymous, and the groups for their friends and spouses such as Al-Anon and Gam-Anon—fosters these feelings.

Craving elevates the dopamine in the nucleus accumbens and conditioned learning elevates the serotonin. This biobalances the brain. Serotonin constrains the ability of patterns to produce a rise of dopamine. The craving ceases.

No longer do we "gotta have" alcohol. After a while, the actual taking of that first drink no longer occurs. The patterns that had produced a craving response for alcohol no longer release dopamine. The craving response for alcohol is extinguished. This is also true for gambling, food, sex, and all other processes that raise dopamine.

The learned conditioned rise in serotonin must be continually reinforced. This keeps our ability to respond to a craving response sharp. If you stop attending AA meetings, the force and the intensity of the conditioned response may not produce sufficient levels of serotonin to biobalance the brain. Not only might this lead to a drinking episode, but the response to alcohol may be reconditioned and the individual will relapse.

It has been observed that those who are successful in AA often increase their intake of coffee, cigarettes, and sweets. Some develop other addictions. This occurs because, while we can stop a particular craving by raising serotonin in a conditioned manner, *the craving brain remains*. What coffee, cigarettes, and sweets have in common is that they unconditionally raise dopamine in the nucleus accumbens and can produce a craving response. As Tom Sabatini said, it's just switching seats on the *Titanic*.

Each craving requires its own conditioned response to raise serotonin. If an ancient reptile was starving a drink of water would not satisfy it. It would need to get food. The primal survival systems produced a craving response that would only be satisfied with that object. The one way to get rid of thirst is to drink. Hungry, got to eat. Crave alcohol. Gotta have alcohol. Crave cocaine. Gotta have cocaine. This explains why we need different organizations for each craving. To condition the rise in serotonin, you must feel the "herd." An alcoholic would not necessarily feel kinship with a sex addict or a gambler or a compulsive eater and vice versa. They do not belong to the same herd. The ability to condition the rise in serotonin is dependent on the feeling of herd. That is why multiple-addicted individuals need to go to the specific group designated for each of their addictions. Sadly, however, no matter how many groups one goes to, the craving brain remains.

"What I get from going to Al-Anon meetings is emotional sobriety," Barbara Levin, a forty-eight-year-old legal secretary, explains. "Fifteen years after the original crisis that brought me there has passed, I still feel privileged to be part of that group. If for some reason I'm forced to miss a few meetings, I can feel the difference in my mood. I become short-tempered, impulsive, and irritable. It's like I need a mental tune-up. What I'm missing isn't anything cognitive, it's spiritual.

"I felt like I was home from the very first meeting I attended. An overwhelming sense of relief and enormous comfort flooded my being. After Al-Anon forced me to look honestly at some of the problematic relationships in my life and helped me accept and deal with them, I was ready to tackle my weight. With the help of Overeater's Anonymous I acknowledged that what I had was an eating problem, not a weight problem. In that room, just like in Al-Anon, there was nothing to explain. Everyone understood how twenty-four-hour grocery stores and two-liter bottles, and fifty-five channels on TV can undermine the best of intentions. We've all been there and we're all committed to keeping each other from going back.

"I've had my current sponsor at Al-Anon for about five years, and I speak to her several times a week. At OA, I am a sponsor for three other members. Many of us belong to more than one twelve-step program. We feel lucky to have cooperated with the miracle. And we are committed to our spiritual maintenance for life."

There are some who attend twelve-step programs who are able to get away from the inescapable stress. The twelve steps can help to change the landscape. The reduction of stress decreases the sensitivity of the nucleus accumbens. The release to a higher power appears to remove the heavy burden of feeling alone. Many report feeling less depressed. Because the inescapable stress that had adaptively lowered their dopamine and serotonin was now being removed, these levels rose, and their depression lifted. Except for these few who have been able to replace their craving landscape, most individuals still own a craving brain. This is why a person is always in recovery and never cured. This is why it is one day at a time.

Nature and AA have shown that we can biobalance the brain in response to a craving. Theoretically then, if we biobalance the craving landscape, we should be able to prevent all perceptions of conditioned patterns from being converted into a craving response. To biobalance the craving brain, we need to increase the landscape levels of dopamine and serotonin. In 1992 Michael Weintraub's research on the use of two medications to raise dopamine and serotonin to control eating behavior did exactly that. It biobalanced the brain. Patients in the study lost weight and were able to maintain that loss while on the medications. These medications, *fenfluramine* and *phentermine*, were known appetite depressants. They not only quieted the appetite but, in our experience, stopped the obsessional thoughts of food and compulsive eating as well as the craving for sweets, carbohydrates, fats, and salt.

Sandy, who discussed her addiction to food in Chapter 1, talks about her reaction to this medication.

"Food has always been the focus of my life. It's like an alcoholic. It's there in your mind. It might not be that you're actively thinking about it at the moment, but it's right there, in the bottom of your brain, encompassing everything. It's very horrifying. It's an awful feeling that wherever I go, I'm going to eat everything that I see.

"There really are some who like the taste of food and they don't care. And there really are some who say, 'I don't know why I can't control this.' That's really who these medications are for, not people who don't work hard enough to lose weight, people for whom it's a disease they can't control.

"After the first month, I said, 'Is this how normal people feel?' I could not believe it. I could see food and I could leave it. In my life, this had never occurred. Even if I'm nauseous, I can eat. If I'm lying in my bed ready to throw up, I can still crave something. It's how I am, the pills control it."

In 1993 Dr. Pietr Hitzig treated a group of alcoholics with phentermine and fenfluramine. He found that the drugs extinguished the craving for alcohol. The pattern recognition processes that produced the craving response were prevented. He had biobalanced the brain.

Nanette Davis, a thirty-four-year-old high school English teacher, has been on the medication for almost a year.

"I've been drinking since I'm like, eleven years old. I would come home from school and fix myself a drink and watch cartoons the way other kids would come home and have milk and cookies. I would open a bottle of wine when I would come home from work at night, have a glass while I was preparing my dinner, then have a glass with my dinner, and, then, proceed to finish the whole bottle. I could not not finish it.

"After two weeks on the pills I had the occasion to go out one night for dinner, and I actually had a glass of wine that I didn't finish—just because I just didn't. I didn't feel like it. I didn't deprive myself, but by the end of the evening, I hadn't even finished one glass. I can go out now and have one glass of wine, one beer, and it's not like I'm saying, 'Okay, I had one. I'll stop.' It's just a feeling of being satisfied, whereas I never had that feeling before.

"It's not like, oh, all of a sudden now I'm more beautiful or I met an amazing man. I'm just happy with me and my life and doing the things that I like to do. I project something different; I can tell; I can feel it. I am different in all social situations. It hasn't altered who I am at all. There's a certain self-confidence. I don't have a crutch; I can count on myself to be an even person. Everybody knows there's no such thing as quick fixes, except this really works."

Tom Krause, who spoke about the tyranny of his addiction to codeine, has also found this type of treatment to be remarkable.

"The day before I started taking the pills, if God came down and said, 'You can flip a coin. Heads you'll be cured, tails you're gonna die,' I would have flipped a coin. That's what stage I was at. Never in my life did I find myself in a situation that I couldn't get out of. Work I hated, but you can get out, leave. Marriage, you can get divorced. But when you're addicted, you can't stop.

"You know what the failure rate on addiction is—ninety-five percent without the aid of a clinic or psychiatrist. You'll hear these clinics in their advertising. Yes, we'll cure you in ninety days. That's the good news. The bad news is eighty percent of you will be back. My God, think of all those people out there who are going through misery. Because it doesn't let up. It doesn't say, 'Well, gee, I'll just come back after dinner.' It's all day, every day.

"Now I've got this craving on a medical basis, there was a problem in my brain. Balancing it puts me in the state I used to be in. I started thinking, maybe your brain is the ruler, you know. Now I can't separate my body from my brain. The brain has become the all-important thing governing my actions. Because two little pills puts everything in order. Is there a God? Did He intervene? I think yes, He did."

Indeed, the power to motivate behavior in response to a need has been refined by Nature over millions of years, along with her ability to cause this behavior to cease. When she determines we have had enough, Nature's solution is to biobalance the brain. To pharmacologically biobalance the brain requires that medication be taken to raise the levels of dopamine and serotonin. We adjust these levels to prevent the pattern recognition and response process from releasing dopamine in the nucleus accumbens. While this sounds straightforward, experience has shown us that other psychological, emotional, and biochemical forces can disrupt the maintenance of the biobalanced state. Once a need is experienced, we are no longer biobalanced and can be motivated to action.

Tom Sabatini's story illustrates how this can occur and suggests that further research into this approach is needed.

"Controversy and chaos is all part of this disease. I lived for the nuttiness and the insanity. It is absolutely part of the high. I picked up my first drink at thirteen. I was smoking pot every day by the time I was fourteen, in junior high school, before school. The first time I ever did speed I was sixteen years old. I went to my first AA meeting at age twenty.

"I had been stoned my whole important years growing up. Then I heard this is all a chemical imbalance. Phentermine and fenfluramine. I took both pills at the beginning. But one of the pills, the fenfluramine, was extremely potent. It made me disoriented and I did not like it. So I stopped taking it. What I did was I kept increasing the dosage of the phentermine." Phentermine is speed, his favorite drug. It raised his dopamine and he felt great.

"I did not pick up a drink or another drug for at least a year and a half after I started taking the pills. I stayed on them for about two and a half years. I was anything but sober. As soon as a mood-altering substance enters my blood system, all choice is over.

"I have stopped now, but I destroyed confidences, trusts, and did a lot of things I would never have done if I didn't reactivate my disease. I have my work-hard attitude on hold. I haven't been able to get the motivation I had back yet. I'm constantly looking for that good feeling of being on top of the world. I'm working my program, doing the best I can. I'm not using, and I don't plan on using, but the craving is driving me insane. I have four months sober. Do I think I'm going to stay clean forever? Eight years ago I would have told you, you know, I really think I am. Today I don't know that."

BIOBALANCE

We propose that one's inherent terrain, hormones, or experience can produce a craving landscape. We can, by raising the levels of dopamine and serotonin, biobalance the brain and prevent the craving response. If, as we believe, pattern recognition and perception are the initiating events for all craving responses, then by altering information processing we can prevent all craving disorders.

The analysis of addictive behavior for alcohol is summarized on the next page. The pattern recognition process leading to a craving response begins by sensing the jingle of ice cubes in a glass. The pattern of sound, conditioned in the past by associative learning, leads the brain to think it will soon be having a glass of scotch. If the nucleus accumbens has been sensitized and serotonin levels are low, the rise of dopamine is great, and we are motivated to get the drink. We crave the drink. After the first drink, the alcohol reaches the brain and causes dopamine levels to increase even more. It is said that the alcohol addict takes the first drink and then drink takes the second drink. Since there is no satiety signal, we continue to drink until we pass out. Nothing can stop that. If this continues, our tolerance will increase, and if we stop, withdrawal symptoms will occur.

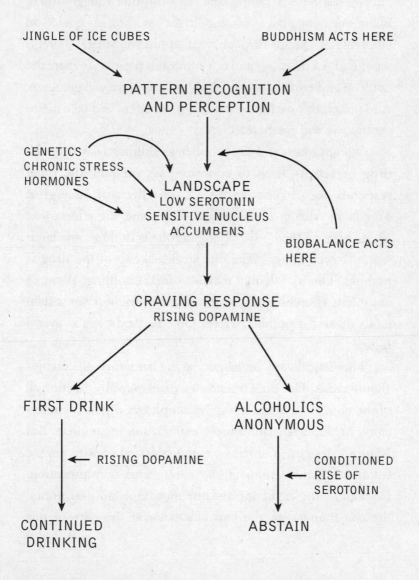

THE CRAVING RESPONSE FOR ALCOHOL

JINGLE OF ICE CUBES

BUDDHISM ACTS HERE

PATTERN RECOGNITION
AND PERCEPTION

GENETICS
CHRONIC STRESS
HORMONES

LANDSCAPE
LOW SEROTONIN
SENSITIVE NUCLEUS
ACCUMBENS

BIOBALANCE ACTS
HERE

CRAVING RESPONSE
RISING DOPAMINE

FIRST DRINK

ALCOHOLICS
ANONYMOUS

RISING DOPAMINE

CONDITIONED
RISE OF
SEROTONIN

CONTINUED
DRINKING

ABSTAIN

It is of no importance which method we use to prevent the craving response. Whether we follow Buddha's suggestion of filling our minds with only the "right" stuff or his advice on emptying our minds through meditation, we will get there. If we attend AA meetings and our serotonin rises as we share the battle of addiction with our fellow sufferers, we will get there. And if each day we follow the doctor's orders and take medications, we will get there.

Our approach sees the problem as shifting away from the drug or activity itself to concentrating on how the brain responds to perception. As Claude Bernard, the great French physiologist, said when discussing the effects that germs have on the body, "The microbe is nothing, the landscape is everything." The chemical makeup of the drug is nothing. The way alcohol makes us feel is nothing. Winning at roulette is nothing. Tasting the world's richest, most delicious dessert is nothing. Here, too, the landscape is everything.

Theoretically, by biobalancing the landscape all cravings should cease. This does not mean we can cure all addiction all of the time. The brain, a highly complex and poorly understood organ, makes any simple explanation incomplete. But Nature's designs, molded over millennia, start with simple solutions to drive motivation, action, and consummation. Dopamine, the facilitator and the motivator, and serotonin, the constrainer, are the two chemicals at the core of this remarkable process. They have provided for enough flexibility to have created our ability to struggle to survive; they can also enslave us. By using Nature's system, we now have a new approach to ending addiction.

6

▼

BIOBALANCE TO MINDFITNESS

The biobalance approach reproduces a state of satiety by raising dopamine and serotonin. Using medications to accomplish this alters the landscape and produces a *heterostasis*.
According to Selye, who first suggested the word, it means a
different (hetero) state (stasis). In addiction, in order to prevent the craving response from occurring, the biobalanced
state, a heterostasis, needs to be continually maintained by
medications. To many, taking medications seemed like a
small price to pay to prevent the craving response. Despite
our early success, however, the drugs were not perfect and
had undesirable side effects. People did not take them and

sometimes their effectiveness waned. Over the last three years, as we began to search for other methods of biobalancing the brain, it occurred to us that if we could reduce chronic stress, the craving brain might be able to heal itself. But how do you escape from an inescapable stressor?

CONSCIOUSNESS AS A CHRONIC STRESSOR

Stress pervades the existence of all creatures. Stressors are considered systemic if they involve the body—for example, hunger, thirst, pain. These stressors have direct access to the stress system and cause release of various substances such as Corticotrophin Releasing Factor, glucocorticoids, noradrenaline, serotonin and peptide hormones such as endorphins. When released, these substances prepare the body to take action. Acutely, they decrease the importance of any unnecessary activity, such as digestion, and set the stage for immediate survival activity. The behavioral and biochemical response to these stressors produces an optimum opportunity to survive.

In addition to systemic stressors, primates and probably other mammals have groups of stressors that are produced by the mind. These are called *processed stressors* (processed by the mind). They also affect the stress system. Through multi-synaptic pathways that evaluate significance to the organism, emotional content, and previous experience, these processed stressors cause the release of the same substances (CRF, nora-drenaline, etc.) as systemic stressors (hunger, pain, etc.). Both systemic stressors and processed stressors can exist in a chronic form with symptoms lasting from months to years to life. If the stressor cannot be eliminated, the body does two things: it adapts so that the individual maximizes the opportunity to find a way to eliminate the stressor, and it reduces the organism's responsiveness to the stressor.

Humans possess a unique awareness that is capable of producing chronic inescapable stress. It is the precursor to an immense class of processed stressors (guilt, worry, anger). It is called consciousness. This self awareness is not innate. For example, a newborn infant cannot distinguish himself from the surroundings (What is that funny handlike thing?). As we mature, we begin to separate from our environment until we are aware of what is me and not me (notably similar to our immune system).

What survival strategy does the development of con-sciousness produce? The simple answer is civilization. Ultimately, civilization led to control over one's survival. Civilization also required controlling our behavior; it required self awareness. From this self awareness comes chronic stress. An almost infinitely long list of inescapable self-made processed (read psychological) stressors, such as fear of death, deadlines, envy, prejudice, and the desire to accumulate things, takes a remarkable toll. A massive collec-tion of illnesses, from asthma to drug addiction, can be linked to chronic life stress and the response it generates in the brain. It seems that civilization may not be a survival bargain after all.

Processed stressors act on the same system as their systemic counterparts. Chronic physical pain (a systemic stressor) produces a similiar response in the stress system as the pain of guilt or loss. Processed stressors are experienced specifically (e.g., guilt, hate, longing) but produce a nonspecific activation of the stress system. You have lost an important promotion to a colleague. You become angry. You want to destroy your competition or the individual who made the decision, but you cannot take action. The inablility to resolve the anger allows for the continuation of civilization but perpetuates a nonspecific stress response and instead causes a depression as the mind tries to protect itself from the chronic anger.

Other regulatory systems also respond to the levels of stress. Each of us has systems which are more or less susceptible to stress. Systems which regulate mood, level of arousal, information processing, and behavioral responsiveness are affected by stress. For the individual described above who lost a promotion, the chronic nonspecific response caused by anger produced his depression. The nonspecific response affected his stress-sensitive system which regulated his mood. For this individual, the depression would have also occurred due to other nonspecific stress responses to ongoing worry over finances or a broken relationship, for example. The response of an individual will ultimately depend on which systems are most susceptible to stress. All of us have systems that drive behavior and are more or less susceptible to stress. This helps explain why stress exacerbates other disorders such as obsessive compulsive disorder, attention deficit disorder, anxiety, and craving.

The important point here is that the processed stressor (guilt, hate, longing) acts in a specific way to produce the feeling and in a nonspecific way on the stress system. These ideas are consistent with the observation that drugs like Prozac can help many people recover from depression despite the varying causes. This is because Prozac works via the nonspecific response system. Thus, if ten people have ten different reasons for their depression, such as the loss of a job, girlfriend, parent, or a lot of money, Prozac, ostensibly, should help them all. It does this by producing a heterostasis in the stress system whereby the response to the stressor is diminished. The stressor no longer activates the stress system and the affected regulatory system returns to a normal state. This also explains why Prozac helps all the disorders where stress plays a role. Psychotherapy also plays an important role if it can reframe the stressor as a neutral, or if it can at least decrease the intensity of the response. Not surprisingly, the limbic system which regulates these processes is involved.

NEOHOMEOSTASIS

While short term stressful life experience can condition long term behavioral changes that have a clear adaptive value to the organism, exposure to an extraordinary stressor, or chronic stressor, can lead to long term maladaptive alterations. Not straying too far from the herd is quickly learned after being chased by a predator. When danger is sensed by a smell in the air or an unusual sound, a learned behavioral response increases the capacity to respond more readily and effectively, and increases the probability of survival. If, on the other hand, a predator was sensed everywhere, the long term response would probably decrease the chance of survival. The body and mind maladapt to the repeated cry of wolf.

In human terms, we can see this in a disorder called Post Traumatic Stress Disorder, PTSD. The chief symptom of PTSD is a heightened response to related events after exposure to a traumatic event. For example, a combat veteran with PTSD hears leaves rustle and finds that his heart automatically begins to race and he becomes hypervigilant, even though he is only walking on the street where he lives. The rustling leaves may also be a backfield stimulus. His response is driven by subconscious connections and a terrain which is hyperresponsive. In addition, there appears to be a progression to increased responsiveness, with the affected individual experiencing more and more of these episodes. Thus, the trauma produced a new state, a *neohomeostasis*: a permanent shift in the reactivity of the stress system. This permanent shift is not a simple adaptation. Adaptations produced by a stressor return to their original state after the stressor is removed (unless irreversible damage has occurred). Here, the initial response to the trauma is a heightened sensitivity to the trauma and the events surrounding it. This increased sensitivity sets the stage for a self-sustaining altered state. PTSD causes a lowering of the threshold to a stress response. Previously neutral stimuli become capable of producing a stress response. In PTSD this continued bombardment keeps the brain in a hypervigilant state.

Chronic, nontraumatic stressors, such as a bad marriage, low self-esteem, or business worries appear to alter the landscape as well, via adaptation to the stressor. Removal of the stressor restores the landscape to its previous functioning state. It is not self-sustaining. Nonetheless, the commonality of PTSD and chronic stressors is that they both influence and are influenced by the stress system.

The observed response to a stressor, or trauma, is a consequence of several factors. These include the intensity and duration of the stressor, the intensity of the response to the stressor (how activated the stress system is), and the reactivity of stress-sensitive systems. These stress-sensitive systems which regulate our mood, anxiety, information processing, and survival behavior, as well as the stress system itself, are homeostatically regulated. That is why we each respond to stress in our own way. This is part of who we are. The ability to decrease stress reactivity by drug or psychological therapy helps all the regulatory systems return to normal functioning. This is currently how we think about treating these problems. Yet, is there another way to accomplish this?

THE BRAIN AS AN ELECTROCHEMICAL ORGAN

For the last fifty years, most physicians and scientists have viewed the brain as a complex soup of chemical reactions. This view led to the idea that the manifestations of mental illness (processing problems) were caused by a chemical imbalance. To accomplish normal functioning, the brain uses hundreds of neurochemicals, which are released by the electrical activity of billions of neurons, to make the thousands of connections needed for each neuron to help us respond to the infinitude of possibilities that life sends our way. In turn, these chemicals regulate the electrical activity of other neurons and, hence, the release of yet another set of neurochemicals and so on. Functional networks of neurons, which are developed gradually under the direction of our genetic code and both conscious and unconscious learning, send information to other parts of the brain, thereby integrating the whole system. It is this interplay between the electrical and the chemical systems that sets the landscape for brain/mind functioning. What is astonishing is that out of this immense complexity certain electrical patterns can be recognized using a technique called electroencephalography (EEG). An EEG is obtained by applying electrodes to the scalp and measuring the electrical activity of the brain tissue below. It is much like an electrocardiogram, which measures the electrical activity of the heart by electrodes placed on the chest. Experts in the field feel that these rhythms reflect the activity of populations of neurons working together. How these networks produce this rhythmic activity is just beginning to be understood.

Since the chemical and electrical systems are related and since it is possible to alter behavior, mood, and information processing with chemicals (drugs), is it possible that by altering brain waves we can also change these systems? This broad question presupposes we can identify what brain waves affect which systems and then are able to alter them. However, for our purposes, we choose to simplify our questioning along two lines. Firstly, can we diminish the nonspecific response of chronic stressors by manipulating brain waves, and secondly, by doing so, can we affect the craving brain?

Research has shown that individuals who suffer from a variety of mental disorders exhibit rhythm abnormalities on their EEG. Thus, one can diagnose or exclude some organic brain or mental disorders based on the characteristics of their EEG. In alcoholism, for example, data suggest that a certain rhythm, called alpha rhythm, is not as active. To explore what this means and what we can do about it requires us to understand some of what we know so far about brain rhythms.

THE ALPHA RHYTHM

In 1929, Berger recorded the first EEG. Using what was, by today's standards, remarkably crude equipment he described what we now call the alpha rhythm. The alpha rhythm is defined as a 8–13 cycles/second oscillation occurring during wakefulness over the back of the head. Alpha rhythms are best observed under conditions of physical relaxation with the eyes closed. The alpha rhythm is diminished or blocked by opening one's eyes. Alpha rhythms are also observed under conditions of profound attention. Archers, when sighting a target, appear to produce an alpha rhythm just prior to releasing the arrow.

Researchers have expended much energy upon correlating personality and psychological traits with the alpha rhythm, but no such correlation has been convincingly demonstrated. Behavioral states, however, have been related to certain alpha rhythms, specifically low levels of arousal and altered states of attention. The areas of the brain which are activated when alpha is generated are the limbic and associated structures on the right side of the brain which feed into the stress response system. The very special conditions of relaxation, dim lighting, and quiet which allow for alpha maximization are rarely found in our daily lives.

THETA RHYTHM

Theta rhythm is believed to be generated in part of the limbic system in a structure called the hippocampus. This 4–8 cycles/second rhythm is active during information processing, as well as selective attention and memory formation. Theta rhythms appear when new and potentially significant information needs to be placed into memory or retrieved. This rhythm is largely under the control of serotonin and *acetylcholine* (another neuromodulator).

As we shall see, it is these two rhythms that open the window to treating the craving brain by altering the response to stressors and helping recondition the mind. The first question to be asked then is can we manipulate them? The answer appears to be yes.

NEUROFEEDBACK

A technique that has been found useful is called neurofeedback. By training to increase alpha rhythms, we appear to produce a nonspecific reduction in the ability of stimuli to produce a stress response. Increasing theta rhythms along with visualizations of desired behavior allows the introduction of new conditioned responses. Neurofeedback is a training tool which allows us to produce specific and nonspecific responses.

Neurofeedback is done in a comfortable sitting position with two earlobe clips and a tiny sensor electrode gelled to the back of the head. The patient's EEG is measured and processed by a computor and the amplitude of desired rhythms is displayed on a screen. A pleasant sound is made when the amplitude of the desired rhythm exceeds a preset number. In 1962, Joseph Kamiya discovered a remarkable phenomenon: when subjects were told that their EEG showed an alpha rhythm, they could eventually learn to control its appearance consciously. Thus, feedback can increase the strength of our alpha rhythm. Other researchers found that individuals who performed this technique and increased the amount of alpha rhythm experienced a sense of peacefulness. Findings on alpha-theta wave training were reported by Green, Green, and Walters, at the Menninger clinic in 1971. They describe the emergence of forgotten memories from childhood and also found that early in treatment subjects felt sluggish, fatigued, or nervous.

In 1989 Peniston and Kulkowsky reported their work on the use of alpha theta neurofeedback in the treatment of alcoholism. Patients were seen five times a week for a duration of four weeks. The Capscan Prism 5 device, developed by Adam Crane and his coworkers to record and to display the EEG, was used. These subjects were instructed to close their eyes and construct visualized abstinence / alcohol rejection scenes, imageries of increased alpha rhythm and normalization of their personalities. Follow-up data taken over a thirteen-month period indicated sustained prevention of relapse in alcoholics that completed brain wave training. This amazing result—that neurofeedback, by altering brain waves, appeared to cure alcoholism—did not gain rapid acceptance. Among the reasons for this is the difficulty in shifting ideas. The reigning chemical imbalance model made so much sense and there was ample clinical data to support it. In addition, brain waves were felt to be so poorly understood as to make them useless for treatment purposes. It is only recently that ideas on how neurofeedback might work are being discussed.

In an article by Othmer, Othmer, and Kaiser, the brain is viewed as a self-regulatory control system; thus psychopathology is seen in terms of specific failure modes of said control system. Othmer refers to this as the dysregulation model. He argues that the regulatory machinery of the brain must be regarded from the bioelectrical, as well as the neurochemical, perspective. Accordingly, for him, much of the basic regulatory activity of the brain is organized by rhythmic activity as seen on the EEG. He feels that using EEG feedback appeals to that regulatory machinery and challenges the control system to become more robust, better organized, tougher, and more resilient. EEG feedback increases the system's capability of returning to a homeostatic balance.

We would like to suggest another idea. Alpha-theta neurofeedback stops the craving response by reducing the level of stress placed on the survival system. Increasing alpha waves decreases the activity of the stress system by decreasing the reactivity of the stress system. This decreased reactivity resets the landscape and diminishes the ability of a stimulus to produce a craving response. If the stress system is less activated, mood disorders, obsessive-compulsive disorders, and levels of anxiety should also improve. This appears to be the case and speaks for the stress system as a unifiying mechanism which affects all these regulatory systems.

By using constructive visualizations during training, such

as rejecting alcohol when at a bar and rewarding oneself for doing so, it is possible to condition the mind to prevent the stimulus from producing a response, in this case a craving for alcohol.

NEOHOMEOSTASIS AND NEUROFEEDBACK

When an individual stops Prozac, unless the stressors have been removed or reframed (a good therapist is critically important here), the original state often returns. In contrast, our experience and that of others suggest that the effects of neurofeedback are long lasting. This is a central finding! An important question then arises: why does not the brain return to its previous state after the neurofeedback training is finished?

We speculate that the observed enduring effect of neurofeedback suggests that it utilizes the systems which aid in the development of lifelong skills through a process called nonassociative learning. Learning to ride a bike is one example of this type of learning. It is impossible to unteach someone to ride a bike once it has been learned.

As Othmer, Othmer, and Kaiser point out, brain rhythms reflect our regulatory machinery. Alpha rhythm generation produces a peaceful state and is associated with the limbic system. By training to increase our alpha rhythm, our stress system becomes homeostatically regulated around a different set point. Thus, instead of increasing the reactivity of the stress system, as occurs in PTSD, neurofeedback decreases the reactivity of the stress system. In both PTSD and neurofeed-back, however, a new self-sustaining landscape is produced. A neohomeostasis is formed.

Sometimes skills need to be replenished, as in the example of learning to ride a bike—it will take a little while to ride as confidently if one has not ridden for years. Research in neurofeedback is in its infancy, but one thing is clear: this technique allows us to reset the stress system and affect many other regulatory systems. This creates mindfitness.

MINDFITNESS

What is mindfitness? The analogy to bodyfitness is inescapable. Mindfitness is the ability to respond to challenges; to sustain an effort; and to respond for the appropriate reason, in the appropriate manner, and for the appropriate amount of time. It is the ability to recover and use resources skillfully. Mindfitness helps us to learn, to explore, and to solve. A fit mind puts you on the road to peak performance. Adam Crane has originated and developed this concept in his program called the Process, a dynamic approach leading to a mind capable of achieving profound attentional states.

For most of us, alpha rhythm training will enhance performance because it can reduce the effect of consciousness. Generally, under long-term stressful conditions, we tend to think more rigidly and are more prone to errors and abnormal thinking. For example, when fatigued, our personalities change and more effort is required to attend to problems. Neurofeedback reduces the reactivity of the stress response system and allows us to reduce errors and be more creative.

If neurofeedback training, and the consequent reduction of stress system activity, is not powerful enough to reset an abnormally functioning regulatory system, medications and psychotherapy should be used in combination. Drugs, psychotherapy, and visualization act differently: the drug on the dysregulated system, psychotherapy on the specific stressor, and visualization to recondition the mind. Other approaches such as meditation, yoga, and neurofeedback which act non-specifically on the stress system can also be added. These approaches require mindfulness, attention by the mind, for learning and change to occur. The development of mindfitness is an active process.

Three years ago, when this book was originally published, we argued that the biobalance approach was the answer to treating addictive behavior. It is clearly only one of the answers. Producing a neohomeostasis by training with neurofeedback is another.

"I was more skeptical than hopeful," Nanette Davis replied when asked about her introduction to neurofeedback. "I had such success with the biobalance program. The drugs worked, but you knew that you were on something and they caused heart problems so the program ended. I started drinking again, gained weight, and my depression got worse, despite medications. For people like me, I'm not a group personality, AA never worked so a sense that this battle had to be fought again made me more depressed.

"I began neurofeedback with thermal training, where you learn to raise the temperature of your fingers. The first day I raised my temperature eight points. This was amazing to me since I always thought it was more difficult to control one's body as opposed to one's behavior. I realized that if I could control something like this, maybe I could control my cravings. My life at this time was a rage thing. I would go ballistic if there was an opportunity. I would throw things across the room, but mostly I'd internalize it. I'd been like this, now only worse, since the age of eleven when my mother got sick and I had to take care of her. I was walking on egg shells every day. It's when I started drinking.

"Carolyn, my neurofeedback instructor, taught me breathing and relaxation techniques and explained how these related to stress. Controlling temperature was easy for me, learning to control my brain waves took about a month. I began to sleep better but was still drinking every night. I trained five days a week but it didn't seem to affect my drinking. My psychiatrist put me on another medication for my depression. Then, there appeared to be a critical point when I learned to control my brain waves, and I started visualizations such as putting my hand over a glass or pouring a glass of wine down the sink. I wanted to stop drinking and did not want the wine in the glass. After the visualization I had a positive feeling. Other issues in my life also became crystal clear.

"I had this dream of flying. I felt so happy, soaring, swooping close to the ground and soaring up again. It was magnificent. I awoke with more confidence, but I was still drinking. Carolyn suggested that maybe I could divert myself after a craving began. I tried walking around the block before I went into the house. It did not take much and my mind shifted. I realized the next day that I did not drink. I still remained skeptical that it was the neurofeedback.

"One day at my father's house, where we always drank, I held the glass of wine, took a sip and poured the wine down the sink. Just like in my visualizations! I realized that this was real life. The training had finished and over the next couple of months I had a glass of beer and some wine, three drinks in three months . . . and it didn't cause me to start drinking again. I knew I would have only one drink. I was sure."

After a short pause, a healthier, thinner, happier Nanette ended her story with "I think I may no longer be an alcoholic."

Mindfitness is not obtained passively. It is obtained by active mindtraining using neurofeedback as a tool. As with any form of training, desire and effort are required. It is important that those who seek mindfitness prepare to change themselves, learn what works for them, and then have the courage and commitment to do it.

7

▼

RESPONSE AND
RESPONSIBILITY

If addictive behavior is irresistibly driven by the craving
response, what responsibility does one have for one's actions?
At what point does the individual lose control? Does the success of some individuals in overcoming addiction imply that
failure to abstain constitutes weakness of character? Or are
some landscapes and conditioning processes simply worse
than others? These are important questions to which we don't
have all the answers.

Our approach does not center solely on abstaining, for
often an addict will abstain many times before the irresistible

urge wins over again. We concentrate on one important goal: making every effort to correct the craving brain. Responsibility for our actions requires a response ability, an ability to say no. The craving response removes the ability to rationally decide our actions. The "gotta have it" is driven by the same overpowering biochemical forces used when survival is at stake. Correcting the craving brain provides choice. With choice comes responsibility for one's actions. While the individual bears primary responsibility, family, friends, and community need to be involved.

For those without an addictive landscape, it is difficult to understand why some people just can't say no. This is especially hard when it comes to understanding craving responses that do not involve drugs. In food addiction, for example, individuals eat enormous quantities of food even when they are not hungry. The addiction is driven by the same landscape that drives the need for drugs. For those individuals whose weight has gone up and down, control over eating today does not mean control tomorrow or next week. Why can't one control food intake tomorrow or next Monday? The answer is that the brain's landscape is dynamic and ever changing. Often what is useful on one day is insufficient to do the job the next. Indeed, it is this drive's very changeability that marks addictive behavior. So for the individual, it has to be one day at a time, or as Tom Krause says, hour by hour. If the craving brain can be corrected, then the craving response, the involuntary "gotta have it," does not occur. Now the individual has a choice. The addict has a response ability.

For example, response ability can be recovered if one's inescapable stress is removed. This was seen after the Vietnam War. Lots of planning went into treating the large numbers of soldiers returning home addicted to heroin. To the surprise of many, few stayed addicted. In fact, follow-up studies revealed their rate of continuing addiction dropped to levels no different from those of the general population. Although 20 percent of the soldiers reported they were addicted to narcotics during the war, only 7 percent said they had used any once they were back home. After ten months, only 5 percent of the original 20 percent still considered themselves addicts, a startling 95 percent remission rate. This was despite their exposure to stress, high-risk environments, and other risk factors that would have predicted a serious addiction problem. When the war was over and they returned home, their chronic inescapable stress was no longer present and they had little trouble leaving their craving behind in the jungle.

Every stressful experience disturbs homeostasis. The change that it generates initiates a response that eventually tries to return the system to its preset range. According to Hans Selye, all stressors, whether they be physiological or psychological, produce the same response. They produce a response that tries to reduce the stress. Physiologically, it's easy to understand. Cold? Seek shelter. Hungry? Get food. The resulting craving landscape makes sense for survival behavior. Take action or perish. Psychological stress deals with our fears and desires, our worries and sorrows. These are often not so readily solved. These stresses can come from either our personal environment or the global environment, from our inner thoughts or from the expressed thoughts of others. Chronic psychological stress, by producing a craving brain, sets the stage for addictive behavior.

It would seem that to change the craving brain, we need to reduce the stress. By altering the pattern recognition process, reducing the sensitivity of the stress system, and providing biologically consonant alternatives to remove the stress, oftentimes the craving brain can be corrected. There are some landscapes and stressors, however, that are too difficult to remedy. Future research may provide us with solutions.

Nature has shown us how to lower the stress produced when we are fearful. She made us herd together, first as families, then as bands, tribes, villages, and finally as entire cultures. It is not geography that makes a culture; it is recognized common patterns such as language and traditions that act as the glue. This bonding reduces the consequences of anxiety through the pattern recognition process of the familiar and friendly. To that end, we fill our lives with many cultures to reduce our fears. The cultures of family, religion, and work all provide a sense of belonging and a commonality of purpose. Culture is a consequence of Nature's trying to help us reduce stress.

For the culture to survive, Nature also gave us the ability to experience feelings of remorse and altruism. These help set

limits and form strong bonds. She gave our minds consciousness to somehow internalize laws by which cultures could survive. She set in our psyches the boundaries of behavior.
Living within these boundaries provides comfort, and feeling
comfort reduces stress. It means we are part of the group.

It is not without consequence that one breaks the boundaries set within a group. Behavior outside the "norm" is
stressful. Addictive behavior is even more so because it is
accompanied by lack of control. The brain adapts and
removes this stress to the subconscious. Statements like,
"What, me an alcoholic?" are honest on a conscious level
because the truth produces distress similar to our inuring
response to forefield stressors like garbage on the street. Even
more powerful, we place this stress in the backfield. We
besome self-unaware. This is the cause of denial. Biologically,
denial can be thought of as a conditioned response to raise
serotonin around the pattern recognition we want to ignore.
Access to this information is constrained, and pattern recognition processes that lead to bringing this to the forefield are
prevented.

Although Nature gave us the ability to reduce distress by
removing it from the forefield to the backfield, she didn't solve
the problem. We know that even though we're not aware of
them, the thoughts and feelings we experience as backfield
pattern recognition also alter the landscape. The process of
backfield pattern recognition of inescapable stress sustains
the increased sensitivity of the nucleus accumbens and

decreases serotonin. This is part of the progressive nature of addictive behavior. The response of the brain to inescapable backfield stress perpetuates the craving brain. This is the process by which unknown demons drive behavior. How can one begin to overcome this?

For the individual, the first responsibility begins with the removal of denial. The importance of this cannot be over-stated. It is the key to beginning the healing process. The subconscious must be made conscious. The admission that a problem exists is entrenched in the philosophy of the twelve-step program. They are the first words uttered at the beginning of the road to recovery. "I am controlled by a craving response," "I am an alcoholic," "I am a gambler," "I am a bulimic." It is the responsibility of the individual who has no choice in his actions to bring this problem to the forefield and seek help.

It seems destructive for a person to be forever labeled as the disease that plagues him. The "I am an alcoholic" stigma-tizes both the individual and the drug. We don't call those who have rheumatoid arthritis rheumatolics, as if they are responsible for the affliction. They have rheumatism. The term *alcoholic* is a poor term for those who have a craving response disorder involving alcohol. They suffer from a condition called alcoholism. This is no small difference. The problem in the literature is that it often casts the abused substance and the abuser as villains. The psychiatric diagnostic manual refers to substance abuse disorders as if it is the substance that needs to be investigated. In truth, as you have seen, the enemy is in us. Assigning a person this label can cause him to lose focus on all else that is positive. This makes it more difficult to remove denial and admit to the problem.

How do we bring a recognition of the addictive behavior to the forefield? Currently, there is no effective way to do this. Interventions where the individual is confronted and placed in an inpatient facility seem to offer little long-term advantage. It is the responsibility of the individual to make that choice, to remove the denial and seek help. Many have to hit bottom, having lost their health, family, job, and self-esteem before admitting that their addictive behavior could no longer be ignored or denied. It is unfortunate that thousands of people find themselves in such straits. If we can prevent the conditioning that created their craving in the first place, we could improve their lives immeasurably. Therefore, it would be extremely useful to be able to unravel the risk factors inherent in the development of the craving brain. Those at high risk could then seek early guidance. The current genetic analysis and the newer brain scanning devices may make this a reality someday. For now, we can look at family history to make us aware of the increased risk.

The second responsibility for the individual is to be actively engaged in the process of correcting and preventing the stress-induced changes that predispose him to a craving brain. Consistent with the concept that the landscape is dynamic and ever changing, this must be a lifelong process.

Current thinking suggests that stress is cumulative, that is, different stresses can add up. This is in line with our experience.

To be actively engaged in reducing stress is of utmost importance. Feeling overwhelmed rather than challenged by the stress in our lives requires action. Active stress reduction can be directed at a particular problem specifically, such as AA meetings or psychotherapy, or nonspecifically, as in meditation, feedback, exercise, or acupuncture. The answer for some might be found in journal writing or taking a nature walk, for others in spending time with one's family, with a pet, or rereading a favorite book. No matter what way you choose, the global reduction in stress will be helpful in reducing the occurrence of the craving brain.

What responsibility does the family unit have in the treatment of this condition? How can they best cope with a loved one who has a craving disorder? Again, the first goal must be directed toward getting the individual to overcome his or her denial. Often this seems like an impossible task, especially if the family member does not believe that there is a problem or that treatment is needed. Those close to the substance abuser must learn ways to handle their own shame and strategies to cope with the stress. Al-Anon, a lay self-help group intended to provide support and guidance for friends and family members of alcohol- and drug-dependent persons, can be helpful in getting over the stigma. These meetings are patterned on the twelve-step program and require first that family members remove their denial as well.

The family unit has a responsibility not just to the afflicted member, but to the unit as a whole. The mood swings, decline in health, and impaired work performance that addicts suffer have an emotional impact on everyone involved. If the individual cannot see a way to seek help, then the family may not survive. This reflects the global destruction addictive behavior can have on a household. We can argue that this condition harms the family and, for its safety and stability, it may need to function separately until treatment for the addicted individual is begun.

The goal and responsibility of any community is to reduce the amount of stress we experience. It is the driving force behind herding and civilization. The conditions we live and work under can be stressful or calming. The pattern recognition of light, noise, and safety, both in the backfield and the forefield, play a role in setting the landscape of the brain. Stressful conditions can lead to a craving brain. Jack Newfield once described Chicago's uptown area: "The tenements are rundown, the hallways smell of urine and many windows are broken. Drunks are folded in grotesque shapes in the doorways. The garbage is uncollected and whiskey bottles wrapped in paper bags seem to grow in every front yard. The fugue of the police siren and the ambulance wail is heard often. Unemployment is about 25 percent." If the image of this inner city is stressful to read, imagine living there.

The culture of poverty, as described by Oscar Lewis, is a response of the poor to this environment. This culture exhibits the consequences of what can happen when a man realizes the improbability of his ever achieving success in terms of the values and goals of the larger society. There is hopelessness and despair in being left out. Owning a home and providing for your children, the bedrock of any culture's economic life, is not possible. Poverty is like quicksand. It can swallow up one's sense of self.

The pattern recognition process of this environment lowers serotonin and increases the sensitivity of the nucleus accumbens to dopamine release. This produces a craving brain. The effects on the individual include a strong feeling of marginality, helplessness, dependency, and inferiority. There is a lack of impulse control and relatively little ability to defer gratification or plan for the future. Children growing up in the culture of poverty know the odds are stacked against them. We see an early initiation into sex, a high incidence of common-law marriages and abandonment, and a trend toward female-centered families. Craving disorders are frequent. They experience academic failure. These problems reflect the response of the brain to chronic inescapable stress. The landscape that is produced drives this behavior. It is a never-ending cycle. Only by altering the environment will we see change.

In our culture, unemployment is stressful. Rewarded work yields a biobalanced state and improves mindfitness. Effort and reward are the foundation of self-esteem. Effort can be equated to the work of a hungry animal as he searches, his dopamine rising, for food. If he expends no effort to get food, say for example he is continually fed by a tube at an appropriate rate, he will never be hungry, nor will he feel full. Similarly, reward without effort cannot produce a biobalanced state. If we do not raise dopamine through effort, then the reward (the consummation, the rise of serotonin) does not biobalance the brain. If there is no discomfort, there can be no contentment, and the learned ability to motivate ourselves is lost. This is why chronic welfare is unsuccessful in achieving its goal. It is why employment is so critical to recovery. Reward without effort is biologically destructive. More important than the wages paid is that effort be heartfelt and recognized in a way that raises serotonin. Begrudging effort does not raise dopamine, nor does the completion of that task raise serotonin.

Other ways of reducing stress and biobalancing the brain include sharing, being compassionate, and "doing good." Altruism, the effort on behalf of another, biobalances us. There is a healing power in doing good. Volunteers who help out on a regular basis report experiencing a "helper's high," a physical feel-good sensation of sudden warmth and increased energy. The end result, peace and contentment, is its own reward.

No discussion of the sources of environmental stress would be complete without mentioning how we are made aware of the world around us. The media shape our outlook and behavior, the values and character of our society. Fewer than five hundred years ago, our daily information was limited to what went on in our village. Now we can scan the globe every twenty minutes. Does the daily portrayal of wartime violence, bread lines, disease, disaster, and downsizing affect us? Does news of flesh-eating bacteria, sex offenders in our neighborhoods, or portraying the black youth as a predator, along with a thousand and one fearful things that can happen to us, alter the nucleus accumbens and serotonin? Of course it does. The pattern recognition process causes stress. We can put this in our backfield, but it still sensitizes our nucleus accumbens and lowers serotonin.

Dopamine rises with images of things that make us anxious. This rise increases their salience. The tag line "If it bleeds it leads" is classic tabloid journalism. The media are aware of this, but disclaim responsibility. Sex, violence, and fearful things catch our attention. These images remain with us, and they become part of our backfield pattern recognition, producing inescapable stress. The media argue that, in the public interest, we should be informed, that change occurs only when information leads to action. But it is only forefield information that leads to change. Backfield pattern recognition of stressful things leads to a craving brain.

How can we solve this dilemma? One answer is to integrate what's positive, what we do right, what's good, with depictions of life's harsher realities. The pattern recognition of the best parts of our culture will reassure us and raise serotonin levels. Our lives would be better if the media could be convinced to biobalance their message. Anxiety-provoking items would raise dopamine, comforting messages would raise serotonin . . . biobalance! Though this idea might sound simplistic, it has its roots in biology.

After decades, our government's war on drugs has yet to win the battle. Billions and billions of dollars have been spent treating and incarcerating those with addictive behavior only to return them to the environments that perpetuate the craving brain. This will never work. The responsibility of government must begin with the creation of biologically consonant policies that provide biobalance and reduce stress. Ideally, these would start before drug use is ever initiated. Since we know the early part of adolescence is a high-risk time for craving disorders, the current trend of toughening the laws restricting and prohibiting the use of tobacco and alcohol for those under twenty-one is encouraging. Conditioning processes learned during this time may be particularly hard to erase. Ninety percent of smokers begin when they are under eighteen years of age. When children who smoke are asked if they see themselves smoking in five years, 75 percent say no. But five years later, 75 percent are still smoking. While prohibition as an adult can never be successful, we can see to it that our children avoid these issues until the end of adolescence, when their brains have adapted to the hormonal challenges. The most powerful weapons in this war are our investments in our children. Head

Start programs, child abuse prevention and enforcement, improving schools, and expanding mentoring programs are not new suggestions, but they are ideas worthy of our best efforts.

We must avoid those biologically dissonant processes that decrease serotonin and increase stress. If, for example, we believe that imprisonment for possession is stressful, then apprehending, prosecuting, and incarcerating a person who already has a craving landscape would only make it worse. If the overall goal of our drug policy is to help substance abusers overcome their addiction, then an argument for the decriminalization of addictive behavior on a biological basis can be made. Locking up dangerous criminals is something the United States does more of than any other nation on earth. But spending millions to build new facilities to isolate addicts from the world they are going to return to, more vulnerable than ever to abusing drugs, is just wrong.

Drugs are here to stay. Certainly, to continue the policy of prohibition makes no sense. It is vain to hope they will ever disappear or that any effort to eliminate them will be successful. The lure of the enormous sums of money earned by those who traffic in illegal drugs is too great. It's basic economics: Where the demand for drugs is strong, an adequate supply will follow. While the drugs that inflict the most harm—nicotine and alcohol—are already legal, introduction of new legal drugs would produce additional problems. A stronger push for drug treatment, rather than incarceration, would help reduce the overall availability of drugs. This approach should not only teach those with a craving brain how to defend against the intricate interplay of biological and psychological factors that fuel their addiction, but just as important, provide for mechanisms that biobalance the brain and improve mind-fitness.

Reducing stress by seeking mindfitness and offering opportunities to biobalance the craving brain are the only biologically sound ways we have of handling addictive behavior. Ultimately and ideally, we need to create the sense that humans are all one herd. That we are all in this together. We need to utilize our biological nature to help alter those processes that lead to disease. "Gotta have it!"

THE SCIENTIFIC FOUNDATION

This section outlines the key scientific data that support the ideas just discussed. Our approach in this section is not just to provide an annotated bibliography from which these concepts have been built, but to offer the reader a glimpse into the scientific process and the experiments that led to this new understanding. Therefore, instead of just listing the sources, we have analyzed their contents. For accuracy and clarity, we sometimes paraphrase short passages from the texts of these articles and books.

CHAPTER 1

1. McFarland, D., ed. *The Oxford Companion to Animal Behavior*. New York: Oxford University Press, 1987.

A clear understanding of how animals behave is available in this storehouse of information readily accessible to the general reader. Written by an international team of experts, it contains over two hundred entries covering a wide range of topics on animal behavior. Descriptions of mating, eating, and fear are included. The way fear is described is particularly illuminating:

> [F]ear is a state of motivation which is aroused by certain specific stimuli and normally gives rise to defensive behavior or escape. Fear provoking stimuli may be "sign stimuli" that are responded to without prior experience, or they may be stimuli to which a fear response has been conditioned. A silhouette resembling a hawk when passed over a duckling induces fear responses when moved in one direction, but not when moved in the opposite direction. Why should this occur?

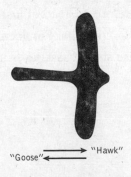

"Goose" ⟷ "Hawk"

Flying in one direction, the short neck and long tail are characteristic of a hawk, whereas flying in the other direction, the long neck and short tail resemble a flying goose. The evidence suggests that some birds have an innate fear of hawk-like configuration since they respond appropriately just after hatching. Primitive, life-saving pattern recognition processing is at work here.

These observations lead us to ask what motivates the animal to action. It is here that the nucleus accumbens becomes central to this discussion.

The following experiments suggest that under appropriate conditions, dopamine rises in the nucleus accumbens when presented with a stimulus that predicts either reward or anxiety. In the survival systems, food and a receptive mate promise peace and contentment. Both the known and the unknown can produce anxiety. It is this rising dopamine in the nucleus accumbens that motivates the individual to action. To understand why this happens, we must look at the survival systems more closely.

2. Willner, P., and J. Scheel-Kruger. *The Mesolimbic Dopamine System: From Motivation to Action.* New York: John Wiley & Sons, 1991.

The survival system consists of several different structures in the brain whose function is to provide for purposeful behavior. The integration of these brain structures and the production of a behavioral response is truly an astonishing feat. The nucleus accumbens, a component of the *mesolimbic dopamine system*, appears to be the key component of the survival system. It connects the limbic system (which tells us what we need) to the motor system (which moves us).

As suggested above, under appropriate conditions dopamine is released in the nucleus accumbens by the same stimuli that activate the whole organism: broadly, incentive stimuli and stressors. Incentives are stimuli that have been associated with primary reward. They predict a certain reward will be delivered if the appropriate action is taken. Stressors similarly require a behavioral response that, if successful, will cause stress reduction. In both cases, the rise of the nucleus accumbens's dopamine appears to be the necessary and sufficient condition for stimuli to produce behavioral activation.

The motivation to action, while driven by the nucleus accumbens, requires an enormous amount of assessment. Recognition of a need is only the beginning of the process that requires an understanding of the risks and benefits of these actions. If the need is great enough, however, actions no longer have consequences.

Incentive stimuli and stressors not only activate but also appear to help organize the appropriate behavioral responses. However, the nucleus accumbens is not involved in the selection of appropriate responses. Rather, its job is to modulate the intensity of the response.

The currently available anatomical information seems to favor the conclusion that the nucleus accumbens mainly operates by parallel processing; that is, by taking in a lot of information and producing a single output that leads to action.

It must be emphasized that motivationally significant patterns (such as food or a receptive mate), in and of themselves, do not lead simply to the activation of a response. They require a landscape that biases perception, potentiates whole classes of response outputs, and alters the balance of our internal physiology. If the nucleus accumbens is sensitized when we see, think of, or smell an object we know will take away the discomfort, dopamine is released and we spring into action.

3. Mitchell, J. B., and A. Gratton. "Involvement of Mesolimbic Dopamine Neurons in Sexual Behaviors: Implications for the Neurobiology of Motivation." *Reviews in the Neurosciences,* 5 (1994): 317–30.

Experiments defining the role of the nucleus accumbens in sexual and food-seeking behaviors are described below. John Mitchell and Alan Gratton describe the recent findings that define the role of the mesolimbic system in the neurobiology of motivation for sexual behavior. The approach they used in their studies was to monitor changes in the levels of dopamine in freely behaving rats using high-speed electrodes planted in the nucleus accumbens.

An inspection of the rat brain reveals a large proportion devoted to the smell system. Thus much of what this rodent learns of its environment is derived from its sense of smell. The experiments consist of monitoring the dopamine levels in <u>sexually experienced male rats</u> when these animals are exposed to three different situations: bedding from cages that housed males, bedding from cages with females with their ovaries removed, and bedding from cages with female rats in estrus. With the electrochemical probe in the nucleus accumbens, they found increases in dopamine coincident only with the investigation of the estrus females' bedding.

> In our studies, nucleus accumbens levels of dopamine increased as the animals explored this bedding and returned to baseline once the stimulus was removed from the testing chamber. This suggests that the rise of dopamine was specific to the stimulus properties of the estrus female bedding. This finding suggests that increased dopamine activity in the nucleus accumbens might facilitate or enable the sequence of purposeful actions that characterize behaviors directed toward rewards. Dopamine underlies the behavioral arousing effect of stimuli that predict the availability of rewards, such as the sight and smell of a receptive female or a food pellet.

4. Phillips, A. G., J. R. Atkinson, J. R. Blackburn, and C. D. Blaha. "Increased Extracellular Dopamine in the Nucleus Accumbens of the Rat Elicited by a Conditional

Stimulus for Food: An Electrochemical Study."
Canadian Journal of Physiology and Pharmacology 71
(1993): 387–93.

It also appears that, for a hungry rat, food can produce
results similar to the effect of a receptive female's odor on a
sexually experienced male. Analysis of changes in the levels of
dopamine showed a significant increase in the nucleus accumbens during the presentation of food. An important factor
influencing the magnitude of the increase appears to be the
degree of food deprivation at the time of testing. The longer
the period of food deprivation, the higher the levels of
dopamine. In contrast, when nondeprived rats were given
access to food, no immediate increases in dopamine were
observed. The landscape on nondeprived animals prevented
a response.

Finally, the response to aversive but not life-threatening
situations may model what happens in the primate brain when
facing an anxiety-provoking situation, such as a novel environment. Placing a clothespin on a rat's tail will not only elicit
clear signs of distress, but will also increase dopamine levels in
the nucleus accumbens. While it may seem paradoxical that
aversive stimuli activate the same dopamine system as
rewarded behavior, it is likely dopamine neurons mediate
behavioral responses to any stimulus of consequence whether
it be the odor of food or a hostile competitor. Thus, similar to
the rise of dopamine when food is presented, a rise in
dopamine is also produced when we confront an anxiety-

provoking situation. It is the system that is activated when action must be taken.

5. Saulskaya, N., and C. A. Marsden. "Conditioned Dopamine Release: Dependence upon N-Methyl-D-Aspartate Receptors." *Neuroscience* 67 (1995): 57–63.

This study investigated the effect of a conditioned emotional response on dopamine release in the nucleus accumbens. The level of dopamine in the nucleus accumbens markedly increased for up to forty minutes when rats were given mild foot shocks in a testing box. When the rats were returned to the testing box and not given foot shock, there was an immediate and long-lasting (eighty minutes) increase in dopamine, which reflected the conditioned response. Since dopamine in the nucleus accumbens rises for food, sex, and fear, it appears that this rise is not linked to any specific state. Thus the nucleus accumbens plays a general role in the survival systems by converting motivation into purposeful action.

CHAPTER 2

1. Betz, B. J. "Some Neurophysiological Aspects of Individual Behavior." *The American Journal of Psychiatry* 136 (1979): 1251–56.

Why are we the way we are? Why do we respond the way we do? Is there a biological substrate of terrain? These questions are addressed by Betz.

The way in which the nerves and chemicals that make up our brain interact constitute an individual's internal domain. This domain is connected to the outside world by two major pathways. The first consists of the aggregate of the nonmotor fibers from the brain to the internal organs of our body. The second consists of the motor fibers that innervate skeletal muscle. Inner events are outwardly expressed as body motions. The individual reveals himself and can be known to others by his characteristic modes of reaction and behavior. Broad stable modes characterizing a given individual may constitute his temperament, a reflection of his biologic "givens."

Feelings generated and experienced in the private domain are simultaneously recorded on the body in the form of movements, as on a public screen. These include and involve emotion, bonding, and self- and species preservation. They are involuntary, so that the individual is continually giving this part of his private domain a public viewing. In humans, conscious efforts must be made to disguise this private emotion from public recognition. In reality, this inside activity and outside activity are two aspects of the same process. Higher-level responses that involve thinking, whose function it is to communicate and interact with the environment, are, to a large degree, voluntary.

Social communication occurs by a wide variety of body signals attentive to the social context—facial expressions, tempo and direction of movement, body attitude, gesture, and sound production refined from lulls and growls to speech and its content. Words and symbols represent physical forces by proxy and are conditioned by experiences within the private domain and by the surrounding culture. The ability to alter the range of responses of one's ordinary functions is crucial for an organism's well-being as an individual and for the social unit as well. This enables him to maintain himself effectively in the stranger-occupied public space around him.

2. Gongwer, M. A., J. M. Murphy, W. J. McBride, L. Lumeng, and T. K. Li. "Regional Brain Contents of Serotonin, Dopamine and Their Metabolites in the Selectively Bred High and Low-Alcohol Drinking Line of Rats." *Alcohol* 6 (1989): 317–20.

Is there something different in the brains of those who exhibit addictive behavior? Li undertook selective breeding of rats to find differences in the physiology of those rats who drank a lot of alcohol compared to those animals who drank significantly less. The first clue to what constitutes addictive behavior was that the alcohol-preferring animals had a different brain chemistry.

Studies on selectively bred rats of the alcohol-preferring (P) line had indicated that ethanol-naive (P) animals have a lower content of serotonin and its primary metabolite, 5-hydroxyindoleacetic acid (*5-HIAA*), in several brain regions (e.g., cerebral cortex, striatum, nucleus accumbens, hippocampus, and hypothalamus) when compared with ethanol-naive rats of the alcohol-nonpreferring (NP) line. These findings were confirmed by breeding another line of alcohol-preferring rats. The regional brain differences in serotonin and dopamine between high- and low-drinking rats were compared to the findings of (P) and (NP) lines. In both cases, brain serotonin was lower in the alcohol-consuming animal.

3. Weiss, F., M. T. Lorang, F. E. Bloom, and G. F. Koob. "Oral Alcohol Self-Administration Stimulates Dopamine Release in the Rat Nucleus Accumbens: Genetic and Motivational Determinants." *Journal of Pharmacology and Experimental Therapeutics* 7 (1993): 250–58.

The second aspect of an addictive landscape was that the nucleus accumbens was more sensitive to releasing dopamine in response to alcohol. Dopamine release in the nucleus accumbens may be an important factor in ethanol reinforcement and genetically determined ethanol preference. This hypothesis was tested by measuring dopamine release in the nucleus accumbens during voluntary oral ethanol administration in alcohol-preferring (P) rats and a control group of normal rats. The animals were trained to respond to either ethanol or water in a free-choice operant task. Dopamine levels in the nucleus accumbens were subsequently monitored during thirty-minute self-administration sessions and a fifteen-minute waiting period before session onset. Ethanol self-administration in all animals was followed by a significant dose-dependent rise in dopamine release with maximal effects at approximately fifteen minutes after peak intake. Dose-effect functions revealed significantly steeper slopes for the dopamine releasing effects of ethanol in (P) than in genetically normal control rats. Over an identical range of ethanol doses and blood alcohol levels, increases in dopamine levels ranged from 143 percent to 459 percent of basal level in (P) rats, but only from 142 percent to 212 percent in normal controls.

4. Cloninger, C. R. "Neurogenetic and Adaptive Mechanism in Alcoholism." *Science* 236 (1987): 410–16.

These above data support the hypothesis proposed by Cloninger that a disposition to alcohol-seeking behavior is associated with biochemical abnormalities. Is this inherent or environmental? Is it nature or nurture? The answer is that it's both.

5. Pickens, R. W., and D. S. Svilkis. "Genetic Influences in Human Substance Abuse." *Journal of Addictive Disorders* 10 (1991): 205–13.

There is a vast literature on the genetic influences of alcoholism and other abused substances. As reviewed by Pickens and Svilkis, a large number of twin studies and adoption studies have been conducted examining quantity and frequency of alcohol use by members of the general population. Recent studies have consistently found that the adopted sons of alcoholics have a higher rate of alcoholism than the adopted sons of nonalcoholics. Two of the three studies with twins found substantially higher rates of alcoholism in identical twins than in fraternal twins. We speculate that these individuals, like the (P) rats, have low serotonin. Does raising serotonin then decrease craving? The cyclical influences of estrogen on serotonin have provided an excellent experimental model for exploring this idea.

6. Brzezinski, A. A., J. J. Wurtman, R. J. Wurtman, R. Gleason, J. Greenfield, and T. Nader. "D-Fenfluramine Suppresses the Increased Calorie and Carbohydrate Intakes and Improves the Mood of Women with Premenstrual Depression." *Obstetrics and Gynecology* 76 (1990): 296–301.

As described by Wurtman and colleagues, blood serotonin levels decreased during the last ten days of the menstrual cycle in women with premenstrual syndrome. PMS is characterized by a high incidence of depression, anxiety, and irritability. In addition, there is often a craving for sweets and carbohydrates, as well as a general increase in appetite. In this regard, these women resemble (P) rats, except instead of alcohol, they desired sweets and carbohydrates. When they were treated with medication that raised their serotonin levels, their carbohydrate cravings and fat intake markedly diminished. The elevated serotonin was also associated with improvement of depression, anxiety, and irritability.

7. Gessa, G. L., A. Tagliamont, P. Tagliamont, P. and B. B. Brodie. "Essential Role of Testosterone in the Sexual Stimulation Induced by P-Chlorophenylalanine in Male Animals." *Nature* 227 (1970): 616–17.

This study reported on the roles of serotonin and the male sexual hormone testosterone in the sexual behavior of rats. Gessa and coworkers found that p-chlorophenylalanine (PCPA), a compound that inhibits the synthesis of serotonin without affecting other neurotransmitters, produces compulsive sexual activity in male animals. This effect was observed in cats, rats, and rabbits. Further, it was found that this effect could be inhibited by restoring brain serotonin levels with 5-hydroxytryptophan, the immediate precursor of serotonin. These workers also discovered that even if the serotonin was low, compulsive sexual activity did not occur in castrated animals. However, when the testosterone was replaced, compulsive sexual activity was restored. These findings indicate that testosterone is essential for sexual activity and that serotonin modulated its intensity.

8. Mitchell, J. B., and J. Stewart. "Effects of Castration, Steroid Replacement and Sexual Experience on Mesolimbic Dopamine and Sexual Behaviors in the Male Rat." *Brain Research* 491 (1989): 116–27.

8a. Mermestein, P. G., and J. B. Becker. "Increases in Extracellular Dopamine in the Nucleus Accumbens and the Striatum of the Female Rat During Paced Copulatory Behavior." *Behavioral Neurosciences* 109 (1995): 354–65.

That dopamine functioning in the nucleus accumbens is affected by testosterone and estrogen was studied by Mitchell and Stewart. These scientists found that the concentrations of dopamine and a dopamine metabolite in the nucleus accumbens decreased after castration, an effect that was avoided by treatment with testosterone or estradiol. These results support the contention that pubertal hormones can affect the level of dopamine in the nucleus accumbens. In addition, the rise in dopamine in the nucleus accumbens in rats where the ovaries had been removed was found to be higher in animals treated with estrogen. Thus the ability of sex hormones to alter the sensitivity of the nucleus accumbens make them landscapers of the brain.

The most speculative part of this theory is the concept of pattern recognition processing. This idea relates to how the brain learns and processes, prioritizes, retrieves, and stores information. The answers to these problems begin with understanding how living things recognize their surroundings. In his article on visual pattern recognition, N. S. Sutherland provided the ground rules needed for investigation.

9. Sutherland, N. S. "Outlines of a Theory of Visual Pattern Recognition in Animals and Man." *Proceedings of the Royal Society B.* 171 (1968): 297–317.

In the late 1960s, research involving recording the brain's response to objects revealed that at the entry parts of the visual system, the input picture is first decomposed into parts, which are then labeled. The retina, the light-sensitive portion of the eye, sends messages on to successive layers of brain cells. At each layer, there are units that fire when a particular feature is present. Researchers refer to this stage of the system as a "processor." They assume that memorizing and recognizing (perceiving) an input shape takes place in a different part of the brain called the "store." In the store, information about input shape is preserved in a form that is independent of its representation on the retina. It is preserved in highly abstract symbols so that many different outputs from the processor can be matched to a single store description of an input pattern.

According to this theory, after a shape is sensed, it is separated into component parts by a preset processor. Recognition corresponds to a successful process of matching the output from the processor to a stored abstract description. Memorizing a new shape corresponds to writing a new description into the store. The two processes are not mutually exclusive. That is to say, when a novel shape is input, a description may be retrieved that partly matches the output from the processor. Thus novel patterns may evoke a response.

The theory assumes that what we see depends upon the rule selected to describe the input pattern. For example, the whole appearance of the Boring (1930) wife-grandmother figure changes when we switch rules. When we see an attractive girl, we are matching the input to a rule describing a young girl looking away. When we switch to seeing an old lady, we are matching to a rule describing an old lady turning toward us.

10. Gazzaniga, M. *Nature's Mind: The Biological Roots of Thinking, Emotions, Sexuality, Language and Intelligence.* New York: Basic Books, 1992.

"Old Woman/Young Woman" by E. G. Boring (1930).
This famous ambiguous figure can be seen alternately as a young woman or an old woman depending on where your eyes fixate. Most people see the old woman first. The young woman is turning away, showing us the left side of her face.

This illusion dramatically demonstrates that what we see on a conscious level is not the pattern on the retina, but the rules to which we match the pattern. How we go about selecting the rule for perception as described above was detailed by Michael Gazzaniga. Dr. Gazzaniga argues that "all we do in life is discover what is already built into our brains. While the environment may shape the way in which any organism develops, it shapes it only as far as preexisting capacities in that organism allow. Thus, the environment selects from the built-in options; it does not modify them." This idea implies that the rule dictates the response. Once a rule has been selected, the perception is fixed. How is the response that comes to consciousness selected? We don't know. The brain scans for connections in the store, looking for similarity. The response depends on the rule selected. From our perspective, it is enough to appreciate that sensation leading to a response is not always under voluntary control.

The pattern recognition and response process becomes even more complicated when we consider the selection from backfield patterns. Subconscious input leads to conscious or subconscious responses. This process reflects the way the brain handles all sensory input, from both outside and inside the body. For example, we are not aware of our feet in our shoes during the course of a day, unless of course they hurt. But our brain is monitoring their every movement, keeping us from falling and helping us respond to the holes in the ground. Thus a sensation that never makes it to consciousness can still be recognized and responded to by our bodies. The science of backfield pattern recognition and response processes has begun to be explored.

11. Spoont, M. R., R. A. Depue, and S. S. Krauss. "Dimensional Measurement of Seasonal Variation in Mood and Behavior." *Psychiatry Research* 39 (1991): 269–84.

Michele Spoont and coworkers describe recent epidemiologic studies that found that the behaviors that characterize seasonal affective disorder (SAD) show seasonal variation in 92 to 95 percent of the general population. This is an example of backfield pattern recognition and response. The winter months, especially in the northern latitudes, bring more darkness. The biologic consequence of less daylight is lower serotonin levels. The behavioral consequences include sugar and chocolate craving (which is why we have chocolate for Valentine's Day in February), weight gain, and depression. The almost universal incidence suggests that seasonal variation in behavior and mood is a continuous dimensional variable extending throughout the entire population. It is defined at the upper extreme as SAD. This illustrates how we are all affected in ways of which we are unaware.

12. Law, S. P. "The Regulation of the Menstrual Cycle and Its Relationship to the Moon." *Acta Obstetrics and Gynecology of Scandinavia* 65, no. 1 (1986): 45–48.

S. P. Law reports on the menstrual cycle and the phases of the moon. Here is another example of backfield pattern recognition affecting another physiological variable. A synchronous relationship between the menstrual cycle and lunar rhythm was confirmed by Law. Among 826 female volunteers between the ages of sixteen and twenty-five with normal menstrual cycles, a large proportion of menstruations occurred around the new moon (28.3 percent). At other times during the lunar month, the proportion of menstruations ranged between 8.5 percent and 12.6 percent. As described by G. Preti, this menstrual synchronization, governed by an as yet unknown backfield pattern recognition process, is also seen in women who room together.

Backfield pattern recognition and response process occurs over all senses and species. It allows a response to occur without conscious intervention. Animals have developed the autonomic nervous system to deal with those backfield processes that can be carried out internally and do not require higher-level functioning. Blood pressure, balance, and temperature are just a few of hundreds of backfield pattern recognition processes that need to be monitored and adjusted.

12a. Preti, G., W. B. Cutter, G. R. Huggins, and H. J. Lawley. "Human Axillary Secretions Influence Women's Menstrual Cycle: The Role of Donor Extract of Females." *Hormones and Behavior* (1986): 474–82.

13. Milders, M. V., and D. I. Perrett. "Recent Developments in the Neurophysiology and Physiology of Face Processing." *Baillieres Clinical Neurology* 2 (1993): 361–88.

The fact that backfield (subconscious) processes can alter physiology is dramatically demonstrated in humans who suffer from a disorder called prosopagnosia. This disorder is characterized by an inability to recognize familiar persons from the sight of their faces. Prosopagnosic patients fail at tasks requiring face naming. Recent evidence suggests that although they might be unaware that a face is known to them, their brains' responses suggest that they do.

This article describes research that showed that for normal subjects, highly familiar faces altered skin conductance responses (much like what is used in the classic lie-detector test). A similar effect was found in prosopagnosic patients. All of these individuals showed higher skin responses to familiar faces, even though three of the four patients were unable to discriminate consciously between the familiar and unfamiliar faces. Thus pattern recognition is a process involving deaggregating input, matching these smaller parts to a "store" based on a selection process already hardwired into the brain. The pattern recognition processes produce a perception, and, depending on the landscape, the brain responds. These processes then affect physiology whether the perception is brought to consciousness or remains subconscious. These articles lead to a new way of looking at the mind. Classic psychoanalytic ideas suggest that particular events produce changes in the brain. While we agree with this, it is also true that day-to-day events, most occurring on a subconscious level, also profoundly affect behavior and mood. Our interactions with the world around us act as stressors. They perturb homeostasis. Ultimately, it is how we deal with the subsequent stress on our systems that determines the outcome of pattern recognition.

14. Selye, H. *The Stress of Life.* New York: McGraw-Hill, 1978.

Various forms of stress give rise to an activation of what Hans Selye calls the *general adaptation syndrome.* To review this landmark work and its implications is not possible here. Suffice it to say that a stressor, whether it be a loud noise or fear or hunger or worry or pain, activates virtually every organ and every chemical reaction in the body, producing a general stress reaction. This stress response is initially nonspecific. Many different types of stressors can produce similar responses. The goal of the body's responses is to return the organism to the state prior to the stressor. For example, when you cut yourself and bleed, your body will make new blood cells to replace those that were lost as soon as the bleeding stops. If it can do this, homeostasis is achieved and the body returns to its baseline state. If the body cannot achieve this, the body does its best to adapt to the situation. If, in the above example, we removed the blood-forming units from the individual and new blood could not be made, the body would adapt to the lowered blood level by initially increasing the heart rate.

The body also adapts by telling the red cells to give up more of their oxygen and by sending blood to the more vital organs. The individual feels none the worse for the lowered blood count. The ability to adapt, especially if the blood loss is slow, is nothing short of remarkable. I have seen people who have slowly lost blood over a period of several months with less than a quarter of their body's blood cells left present with relatively mild symptoms. These two processes, the acute attempt to return to equilibrium and the adaptation to chronic conditions, typify the response to stress. The third phase of this process is exhaustion, a condition that leads to the death of the organism. If the blood loss persists, the individual becomes weaker. Ultimately, despite all adaptations, there is not enough blood to maintain the integrity of the body, and the individual dies.

Selye believed that the perpetual attempt at *adaptation* leads to disease. The heart has to pump harder and the bone marrow has to work harder to make blood. Eventually, the body can no longer sustain the effort. In essence, disease is a late manifestation of an imbalance, an inescapable stress producing attempts at restoring homeostasis. When this is prolonged, we run out of what Selye calls "adaptation energy," and our body starts to fall apart. Generally, the stress response was meant to be acute or at least of limited duration. The time-limited nature of this process renders its accompanying increased breakdown of vital tissues of little consequence. Adaptations are designed to increase the probability of survival from the stressor so that at some future time the adaptation may not be needed. However, adaptations, if prolonged, will ultimately produce disease.

14a. Chrousos, G. P., and P. W. Gold. "Stress and Stress Disorders." *Journal of the American Medical Association* 267 (1992): 1244–52.

As described by Selye and reviewed by Chrousos and Gold, the secretion of glucocorticoids is the cornerstone of the stress response. The response to chronic stress appears to be involved in the following: melancholic depression, anorexia nervosa, panic disorder, obsessive-compulsive disorder, decreased resistance to infection, chronic alcoholism, premenstrual syndrome, or vulnerability to addiction. While the stressor can be nonspecific—for example, anxiety—the disorder it produces occurs at the site of the weakest link. For some people it's their stomach, for others their heart, while for others, stress is reflected in a dysfunctional mind.

15. Rouge-Pont, F., M. Marinelli, M. LeMoal, H. Simon, and P. V. Piazza. "Stress Induced Sensitization and Glucocorticoids: Sensitization of the Increase in Extracellular Dopamine Induced by Cocaine Depends on Stress-Induced Corticosterone Secretion." *Journal of Neuroscience* 15 (1995): 7189–95.

Glucocorticoids seem to control the stress-induced sensitization of the behavioral effects of abused drugs by acting on mesolimbic dopamine transmission and increasing the sensitivity of the nucleus accumbens. In experiments carried out by Dr. F. Rouge-Pont and coworkers, concentrations of dopamine were evaluated in the nucleus accumbens of freely moving animals. Metyrapone, an inhibitor of glucocorticoid synthesis, was used to block its stress-induced production. Food restriction (up to 90 percent of the initial body weight) was the stressor used to induce sensitization. In the experiment, rats were either treated or not treated with metyrapone. The baseline levels of dopamine in the nucleus accumbens after food restriction were the same for both the metyrapone-treated and metyrapone-untreated animals. The levels were also identical to those of animals that were not food restricted. The rats were then given cocaine, and the level of dopamine in the nucleus accumbens was measured. The increase in dopamine for both the metyrapone-treated group and the group that could eat as much as it wanted was identical (approximately 225 percent above baseline). The food-restricted group without metyrapone treatment when given cocaine produced a 325 percent increase from baseline. In other words, if the glucocorticoid is not available, the nucleus accumbens cannot be sensitized by stressors to release more dopamine.

16. Kitayama, I., A. Cintra, A. M. Janson, K. Fuxe, L. F. Agnati, P. Eneroth, M. Aronsson, A. Aarfstrand, H. W. M. Steinbush, T. J. Visser, M. Goldstein, W. Vale, and J. A. Gustafsson. "Chronic Immobilization Stress: Evidence for Decreases of Serotonin Immunoreactivity and for Increases of Glucocorticoid Receptor Immunoreactivity in Various Brain Regions of the Rat." *Journal of Neural Transmission* 77 (1989): 93–130.

Thus stress is produced by both backfield and forefield pattern recognition processes and mediated through the release of glucocorticoids. Brain dopamine and serotonin neurons have also been found to be altered by acute and chronic stress, and it is possible that these effects are mediated at least partially through glucocorticoids.

Kitayama and coworkers showed that when male rats were exposed to severe fourteen-day immobilization stress, changes in serotonin occurred. Seven days following cessation of the chronic stress, total locomotion and forward locomotion, both measures of dopamine function, were restored to normal. Serum cortisol levels appeared to remain high even six days following cessation. The reduction of serotonin in various serotonin cell groups indicates a reduction of serotonin synthesis that may also be associated with reduced serotonin release from nerve terminals.

These animal experiments suggest that inescapable or unpredictable stress reduces brain serotonin and increases the sensitivity of the nucleus accumbens. Accordingly, if inescapable stress appears to produce a craving landscape, the animal should increase alcohol intake. This study, carried out from a behavioral point of view by Nash and Maicke, investigated the response that stress produced on alcohol intake.

17. Nash, J. F., and R. P. Maicke. "Stress-induced Consumption of Ethanol by Rats." *Life Sciences* 37 (1985): 757–65.

Rats were maintained on a continuous choice situation for consumption of either 0.1 percent aqueous saccharin or 10 percent ethanol/0.1 percent saccharin. After a stabilized base-line was achieved, the rats were divided into three groups. They were exposed either to no stress, to an unpredictable schedule of isolation, or to immobilization stress for fourteen days. <u>Upon cessation of the stress exposures</u>, the isolation and immobilization groups markedly increased their consumption of ethanol solution.

This unpredictability reflects the stresses of everyday human life. Most of us have had to "keep it together" during periods of stress, only to experience the consequences of the stress later on. At the end of a hard day, we look forward to that drink at night.

Human existence, even for those living with inescapable stress, is made up of periods of greater stress alternating with periods of less stress. Thus, while day-to-day struggles do not in and of themselves produce addictive behavior, they appear to landscape the brain so that when our focus on the stressor is gone, the pattern recognition processes that lead to drinking can now occur. These stressors come from within ourselves and our culture, from the forefield or the backfield.

18. Bales, R. F. "Cultural Differences in Rates of Alcoholism." *Quarterly Journal of Studies in Alcohol* (1946): 480–99.

Since the pioneering work of R. F. Bales, stress has been suspected of affecting the consumption of alcohol in humans. Based on his sociological research, Bales postulated that the rate of alcoholism in certain cultures or societies correlates with its levels of stress (tension and frustration). He concluded that the level of alcohol use was dependent on factors such as cultural supports, attitudes toward alcohol ingestion and intoxication, and whether there were alternate mechanisms to relieve stress.

Other theories focus on the causal factors within the motivation of the individual alcoholic. Stressors such as divorce, unemployment, illness, and isolation all add to the risk of alcoholism. <u>It is postulated that what's critical is not so much the content of the separate stressors, but the culmination of stressful events that characterize the social environment</u>. This is consistent with the idea that different stressors (worry, anxiety, depression, loss) produce similar changes in the brain, and that they can be cumulative. All of this research has one problem. It is often difficult to say when an individual has just increased his use of alcohol and when he is developing addictive behavior. However, stress on an appropriate landscape can, in actuality, produce addictive behavior. This is dramatically seen in Native Americans.

19. Mail, P. D. "American Indians, Stress and Alcohol." *American Indian and Alaska Native Mental Health Research* 3 (1989): 7–26.

The Native American culture that has been devastated by alcoholism was reviewed by Patricia Mail. Her conclusions are applicable to any culture that has been subject to deculturation and acculturation stress.

Stress that contributes to addictive behavior is often described as resulting from deviant cultural change, either too rapid acculturation or deculturation. Acculturation stress is the result of the demands to integrate into and identify with another more dominant culture. Deculturation stress is that resulting from the loss or devaluation of historical tradition. The Native American has suffered from both of these processes. This has led to family disruption. It is surmised that the most common precipitating cause of child abuse and neglect is the extreme social stress experienced by parents who lack effective supports and coping mechanisms. Observed patterns of maltreatment among Native Americans resulted from such factors as sibling caretaking, poverty, a generation of unparented parents, alcoholism, and situational stress with ineffective social supports. These processes lead to chronic inescapable stress because there is no safe place to be.

In summary, the research and experimental data show that the nucleus accumbens releases more dopamine in animals who prefer alcohol and in animals who are stressed. It reveals that the pubertal hormones—testosterone and estrogen—have effects beyond those of simply driving sexual behavior. It demonstrates a role for serotonin in both craving behavior and *compulsive behavior*. Therefore, some people, sometimes, under some circumstances will develop an addiction. It remains for us to show how this research can be applied to understanding and treating this behavior.

CHAPTER 3

What drives addictive behavior? We speculate that biological processes produce involuntary responses that make one "gotta have it." This behavior is also associated with other involuntary responses. Understanding the physiology of the associated responses was first explored by Pavlov almost a century ago. In a typical Pavlovian experiment, food is presented to a hungry dog. The dog's mind says "gotta have it." The dog salivates. At the next feeding, a bell is rung immediately before the presentation of food. The dog salivates. After several trials, the bell is rung without the presentation of food. It is observed that the dog salivates in response to just the bell. Pavlov termed the food the unconditioned stimulus and the sound of the bell the conditioned stimulus. The salivation in response to the sight of food was the unconditioned response and the salivation to the bell alone the conditioned response. In truth, salivation in response to the sight of the food was also a conditioned response.

Pavlov found that it was much easier to form a conditioned response if the unconditional stimulus (food) was presented after the conditional stimulus (bell). A dog will salivate more if he is trained with a bigger piece of food or a louder bell.

The animal learned to discriminate between signals. A horn would not elicit as much salivation as the bell to which it was conditioned. Pavlov was also interested in how the animal lost its ability to respond. He classified the factors causing the loss of a conditioned response into cases of either external inhibition or internal inhibition. If an animal, conditioned in a certain environment, was transferred to a new environment, it lost its ability to respond to the conditioned stimulus (external inhibition). The ability to respond to a stimulus can also be lost by not rewarding, that is, withholding food after the bell is rung. The conditioned response (salivation) requires regular reinforcement by the unconditional stimulus (food). These concepts will be valuable in further research on addictive behavior.

1. Jacobs, W. J., and J. R. Blackburn. "A Model of Pavlovian Conditioning: Variations in the Representation of the Unconditional Stimulus." *Integrative Physiological and Behavioral Science* 30 (1995): 12–33.

Interestingly, Pavlov reported on a phenomenon known as "reinstatement." Following conditioning, repeated unrewarded presentations of the conditional stimulus (the bell) alone results in behavior extinction (internal inhibition). The bell can no longer by itself elicit salivation. Subsequently, responding to the bell can be reinstated by a single, noncontingent presentation of the food in the experimental environment. The animal that had not initially responded to the bell because of behavior extinction can be made to respond again by only a single representation of the unconditioned stimulus. This means that if we provide food in the proper setting even after the salivation response to the bell has been extinguished by nonreinforcement, the animal will, at a later date, respond to the bell again. The implication here for alcoholics is that even one drink (unconditioned stimulus) under the correct conditions can reinstate the ability of a conditioned stimuli to produce the craving response. Therefore, we cannot extinguish the craving response simply by not rewarding it. It is important to note that there are, however, mechanisms that can truly extinguish the conditioned response. These ideas will become useful when we discuss cue reduction techniques.

Finally, the critical experiment. If a conditioned dog was fed just prior to ringing the bell, would salivation occur? The answer is no. This is similar to our own life's experience. If we are hungry and sit down to eat, we salivate. If, after a full meal, we are presented with the identical food again, we are uninterested and do not salivate. The brain is biobalanced for food, and the involuntary physiological responses do not occur. The landscape had changed.

Early theories on the causes of drug addiction began with the concepts of conditioning. This was central to Wikler's classic article on addiction.

2. Wikler, A. "Conditioning Factors in Opiate Addiction and Relapse." In D. I. Wilner and G. C. Kassebaum, eds. *Narcotics*. New York: McGraw-Hill, 1965. (See also Wikler, A. *Journal of Substance Abuse Treatment* 1 [1984]: 277–85.)

Wikler postulated that a craving response may become conditioned to environmental situations specifically associated with availability of the drug. He believed that "absti-nence distress," or something very much like it, may be reac-tivated long after "cure." If the post-addict finds himself in a situation similar to where he practiced his previous drug-using activities, that environment can provide an uncon-scious motivation to relapse and renewed self-maintenance of addiction. Wikler stated that "just as salivation and increased appetite or hunger can be evoked by sight of food, a condi-tioned withdrawal syndrome with associated craving may result whenever the alcoholic passes a bar, sees other people drinking, or encounters cues relevant to previous drinking episodes." These cues were studied by Ludwig and are described in this book.

3. Ludwig, A. M. "Pavlov's 'Bells' and Alcohol Craving." *Addictive Behaviors* 11 (1986): 87–91.

4. Ludwig, A. M., and L. H. Stark. "The First Drink: Psychobiological Aspects of Craving." *Archives of General Psychiatry* 30 (1974): 539–47.

Wikler and Ludwig further proposed that anxiety, ner-vousness, and other types of emotional *dysphoria* may pro-duce physiological responses such as increased heart rate and respiration, tremulousness, autonomic liability, increased sweating, and insomnia, all of which represent changes asso-ciated with alcohol withdrawal syndrome. We should antici-pate that these states induced by either argument, employment difficulties, or loneliness may likewise evoke craving. The authors quote Tokar et al. ("Emotional States and Behavior Patterns in Alcoholics and Non-Alcoholics." *Quarterly Journal for the Study of Alcohol* [March 1973]: 133–43), who report that "alcoholics, in comparison to normal controls, are more likely to go to the bar, drink booze, smoke, and take pills whenever they feel helpless, depressed, angry or anxious."

The removal of physical distress has been suggested as the mechanism that sustains addictive behavior. Ludwig and Stark postulate that the first drink, under appropriate conditions, reproduces the entire sequence of behaviors demonstrated in previous drinking episodes. They argue that only by continued drinking will the subclinical discomfort of withdrawal be alleviated. This early research focused on narcotics and alcohol, both of which produce clear tolerance and physical withdrawal symptoms. Addictive drugs that do not produce withdrawal symptoms were thought to act by alleviating the "psychological distress syndrome," which is a depressed mood and dysphoria produced by discontinuation of the drug. The idea that distress, whether physical or psychological, drives addictive behavior has been reviewed by Robinson and Berridge and has largely been discounted.

5. Robinson , T. E., and K. C. Berridge. "The Neural Basis of Drug Craving: An Incentive-Sensitization Theory of Addiction." *Brain Research Reviews* 18 (1993): 247–91.

The theory that individuals are addicted to the pleasurable experience of the drug has also been studied. It seems unlikely that the subjective pleasure of the drug itself is sufficient to produce addictive behavior. Robinson and Berridge again review the data. They state that there is no clear relationship between the ability of individual drugs to produce euphoria and their addictive potential. For example, nicotine is considered highly addictive, but it does not produce marked euphoria or other strong hedonic states. In fact, to most people, including addicts, the negative consequences of continued drug use are enormous relative to the pleasure derived from the drugs. If you can become addicted to a substance that does not decrease stress or provide pleasure, it is difficult to explain a number of important features of addictive behavior. Specifically, an adequate theory of addiction must explain the following:

1. What accounts for drug craving?

2. Why are only certain substances and activities abused?

3. Why does obsessive craving persist in the face of enormous negative consequences?

4. Why is relapse so prevalent?

5. Why can relapse be precipitated by so many different stimuli?

Robinson and Berridge view the drug as the center of addiction. They believe that addictive behavior results from an adaptation of the nucleus accumbens to chronic drug use, making it more sensitive. In other words, giving the drug repeatedly enhances dopamine release. There are conflicting data in this regard. They also submit that dopamine release makes the drug "wanted," in essence, makes one crave the drug.

6. DiChiara, G., E. Acquas, G. Tanda, and C. Cadoni. "Drugs of Abuse: Biochemical Surrogates of Natural Rewards?" *Biochemical Society Symposia/Biochemical Society* 59 (1993): 65–81.

7. DiChiara, G. "The Role of Dopamine in Drug Abuse Viewed from the Perspective of Its Role in Motivation." *Drug and Alcohol Dependence* 38 (1995): 99–137.

Recently, the study of biochemical mechanisms in the brain has led to several theories about addictive behavior. DiChiara has found that pharmacological as well as biochemical studies performed with brain microdialysis in freely moving rats suggest that many drugs of abuse mimic the incentive properties of natural rewards. That is, they raise dopamine in the nucleus accumbens. While this conclusion is widely agreed upon, its interpretation is open for discussion.

Although drugs of abuse belong to different pharmacological classes (morphine and methadone are narcotics; alcohol is a central nervous system depressant; amphetamines, cocaine, and phencyclidine are psychostimulants; and nicotine is a cholinergic *agonist*), they all increase dopamine levels in the nucleus accumbens. How this happens differs, depending on the drug. "Some drugs inhibit uptake of dopamine, some increase the firing of stimulating neurons, while others directly release additional dopamine."

Another feature these drugs of abuse have in common is that they stimulate motor activity. They also facilitate intracranial self-stimulation (ICSS), a process thought to be related to enhancing the rewards of the drug and one that requires an intact dopamine system. Withdrawal from these drugs of abuse results in a decrease of dopamine in the nucleus accumbens and may drive behavior to replenish the dopamine level. While these observations suggest that dopamine is somehow involved with the abuse liability of drugs, DiChiara and coworkers felt that the mechanism for drug abuse and addiction cannot be accommodated by a single neurotransmitter hypothesis. For these researchers the exact role played by dopamine remains unclear.

Our view is that changes in brain receptors induced by drugs may represent an adaptation leading to the development of tolerance and withdrawal symptoms. We postulate that they have little to do with the craving response. The idea that the drug itself is not critical to the development of addiction is confirmed in Chapter 7 where we describe the Vietnam veteran experience.

8. Tihonen, J., J. Kuikka, K. Bergstrom, P. Kakola, J. Kahu, O. P. Ryynanen, and J. P. Fohr. "Altered Striatal Dopamine Reuptake Site Densities in Habitually Violent and Non Violent Alcoholics." *Nature Medicine* 1 (1995): 654–57.

More recently, data on dopamine receptors have suggested that the density of dopamine transporter sites were markedly lower in nonviolent alcoholics than in violent alcoholics or healthy controls, suggesting that a deficiency of dopamine transmission underlies certain types of addictive behavior. Based on these studies, Cloninger presents a neurogenetic model of alcohol subtypes (see next page).

A neurogenetic model of alcohol subtypes

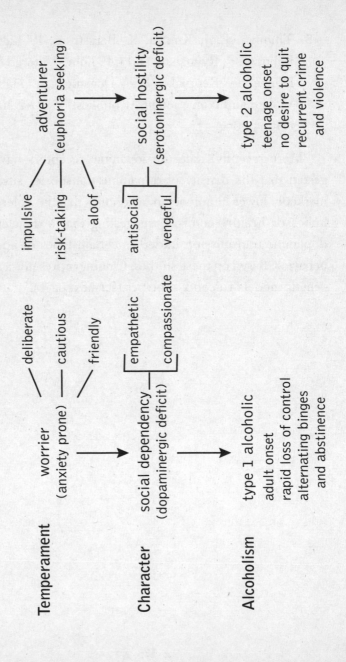

Temperament

worrier
(anxiety prone)

— deliberate

— cautious

— friendly

adventurer
(euphoria seeking)

— impulsive

— risk-taking

— aloof

Character

social dependency
(dopaminergic deficit)

empathetic

compassionate

social hostility
(serotoninergic deficit)

antisocial

vengeful

Alcoholism

type 1 alcoholic
adult onset
rapid loss of control
alternating binges
and abstinence

type 2 alcoholic
teenage onset
no desire to quit
recurrent crime
and violence

9. Cloninger, C. R. "The Psychobiological Regulation of Social Cooperation." *Nature Medicine* 1 (1995): 623–24.

He suggests that one kind of alcoholism (which he calls type 1) reflects a dopaminergic deficit, and another kind (which he calls type 2), a serotinergic deficit. According to his analysis, the type-1 alcoholic experiences alternating binges and abstinences.

Cloninger also points out that when serotonin turnover in the brain is low, dopamine turnover is likely to be low as well. When the serotonin increases, there appears to be an increase in the dopamine metabolite, suggesting that serotonin facilitates dopamine release. This becomes important when we explore the role of Alcoholics Anonymous.

Our view is that the individual is motivated when dopamine is raised in the nucleus accumbens. Addictive and compulsive behavior occur not just because of the rise of dopamine in the nucleus accumbens, but because of the low level of landscape serotonin. Some drugs of abuse such as narcotics, nicotine, and cocaine rapidly raise dopamine and serotonin. Other drugs like alcohol and activities like gambling do not cause a concomitant rapid rise in serotonin. This difference is reflected in their patterns of abuse. On ingestion, narcotics will stop drug-seeking behavior. One drink of alcohol for an alcoholic, however, produces a binge.

10. Zhou, Z. F., and J. S. Han. "Studies on the Mesolimbic Loop of Antinociception-II: A Serotonin-Enkephalin Interaction in the Nucleus Accumbens." *Neuroscience* 19 (1986): 403-9.

11. Broderick, P. A. "Opiate Regulation of Mesolimbic Serotonin Release: In Vivo Semiderivative Electrochemical Analyses." *Neuropeptides* 5 (1985): 587-90.

12. Yu, Z. J., and L. Wecker. "Chronic Nicotine Administration Differentially Affects Neurotransmitter Release from Rat Striatal Slices." *Journal of Neurochemistry* 63 (1994): 186-94.

13. Parsons, L. H., and J. B. Justice, Jr. "Serotonin and Dopamine Sensitization in the Nucleus Accumbens, Ventral Tegmental Area, and Dorsal Raphe Nucleus Following Repeated Cocaine Administration." *Journal of Neurochemistry* 61 (1993): 1611-19.

Compulsive activities, such as gambling, food bingeing, and alcoholism where the behaviors continue until one runs out of money, the stomach gets filled to capacity, or the direct CNS depressant effect of alcohol causes the individual to pass out, produce either a delayed rise in serotonin or no rise at all. This may be why these activities, once they begin, are difficult to stop. Dopamine is unopposed by serotonin. Addictive and compulsive activities are initiated by the same process: a rise of dopamine in the nucleus accumbens. For these behaviors, drinking alcohol (compulsive drug taking) to gambling (compulsive betting) reflect the brain's primitive biological response to try to biobalance itself. We are motivated to action.

Critical to the understanding of the biobalance theory is the dual role that dopamine plays. Dopamine's rise in the nucleus accumbens converts landscaped perception into responses (motivation to action). Dopamine also rises in other parts of the brain to enable the acquisition of incentive properties of patterns (conditioned learning) and govern the level of arousal and sharpness with which we view the world. These roles, motivator and modulator, represent the *phasic/synaptic* mode of dopamine transmission and *tonic/nonsynaptic* role, respectively. The phasic role is represented by acute rises in nucleus accumbens dopamine when a pattern recognition process produces this response. The second role, the tonic role, reflects the day-to-day levels of dopamine in the brain. High dopamine makes us feel good. It allows us to learn and think clearly and increases our ability to make associations. Low dopamine makes us tired and depressed. At the end of a long day, as we begin to run out of dopamine, we feel tired and think less clearly. After a good night's rest, when our dopamine is restored, we feel and think more brightly and clearly. A theory of dopamine and its roles are outlined by Cohen and Servan-Schreiber.

14. Cohen, J. D., and D. Servan-Schreiber. "A Theory of Dopamine Function and Its Role in Cognitive Deficits in Schizophrenia." *Schizophrenia Bulletin* 19 (1993): 85–104.

In primate brains, neurons containing dopamine originate in the most ancient area of the brain, called the mesencephalon. Two parts of this area, the substantia nigra and the tegmentum, send fibers diffusely to motor and higher functioning associational areas in the brain (see figure below). The

DOPAMINE PROJECTIONS IN THE BRAIN

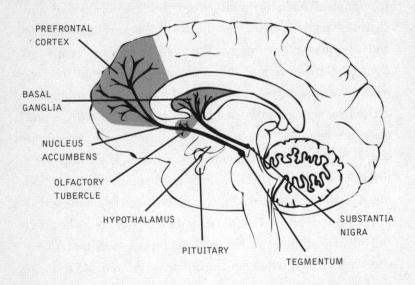

Dopamine projections begin in the substantia nigra (which leads to the basal ganglia and controls movement) and the tegmentum (which leads to the nucleus accumbens and prefrontal cortex and controls motivation).

pattern of these *projections* is distinct from that of other primitive systems that involve projections to sharply delineated areas of the brain. Dopamine projections are distributed in a tangential fashion. They intersect topographically organized thalamic projections and branch profusely along the surface of the cortex. A single axon from a dopamine neuron may therefore traverse several functionally distinct regions. This anatomical organization is well suited to a diffuse, modulatory action rather than to a spatially precise transmission of discrete sensory and motor signals.

The details of the effects of dopamine on learning are well beyond the scope of this book. However, the model developed in the above article shows that an important consequence of dopamine's cellular effects may be to affect the quality of the signal represented over a network of cells. That is, it increases the signal-to-noise ratio, making the object of conscious focus more salient and facilitating associative processes. This action is independent of the function dopamine plays in the nucleus accumbens. In conditioned reinforcement, learning is facilitated by psychostimulants, which raise dopamine. That is, they increase our ability to learn. These researchers believe that dopamine is critical not to the process of specific-stimulus learning, but rather to increasing response associations.

These two roles, dopamine as the motivator to action that is played out in the nucleus accumbens (the phasic/synaptic role) and its role in information processing and general level of arousal (the tonic/modulating role) are the key brain functions of dopamine.

15. Beninger, R. J. "The Role of Dopamine in Locomotor Activity and Learning." *Brain Research Reviews* 6 (1983): 173-96.

16. Spoont, M. R. "Modulatory Role of Serotonin in Neural Information Processing: Implications for Human Psychopathology." *Psychological Bulletin* 112 (1992): 330-50.

If dopamine facilitates associative processes, serotonin constrains them. If dopamine motivates action, serotonin asks for calm. If dopamine makes us impatient, serotonin allows for patience. Like dopamine, serotonin has two functions. The dual aspects of serotonin function are brilliantly synthesized by Michelle Spoont.

Imagine a state such as severe hunger. The stress system heightens the responsiveness of the nucleus accumbens. Dopamine is raised in the associational areas of the brain. The first sight, smell, or sound of food releases dopamine in the nucleus accumbens and motivates action to obtain it. After eating, serotonin rises acutely. This is the phasic function of serotonin. Along with dopamine, it creates a sense of satiety that decreases associative processes and inhibits motivated behavior for that process for which the action has been completed. In the phasic/synaptic roles, dopamine is the "gotta have it" and serotonin is the "got it."

Serotonin plays a role in the modulatory aspects of information processing as well. Dopamine allows for switching of responses to occur. That is, if we are looking for food, dopamine will make us look everywhere. Too much dopamine makes the search frenetic and purposeless. The tonic level of serotonin constrains switching responses. Except at abnormally high levels of serotonin, inhibition of the switching function of dopamine is not completely restrained. Rather, serotonin attenuates this activity so that controlled behavioral output (as opposed to unmitigated switching) results. This allows us to focus.

Retrieval of information, which is another form of associative processing, is facilitated by either increased dopamine or decreased serotonin. Under chronic stress, the brain must seek out any solution. Therefore, serotonin is lowered and allows for more connections to be made. These are the fine balances between dopamine and serotonin in neural information processing.

As we understand it, the craving response occurs because (1) associative processes facilitated by a higher tonic level of dopamine can be conditioned to reproduce the rise in dopamine in the nucleus accumbens for drugs and activities that raise dopamine, and (2) the nucleus accumbens is sensitized to release dopamine (the synaptic role) and the serotonin is low (the tonic role). <u>The craving response ceases when both the dopamine and serotonin levels are raised.</u> Thus we see how the dual roles of dopamine and serotonin affect learning, motivation, action, and cessation of the craving response.

CHAPTER 4

The discussions on Buddhism, the discovery of addiction, and Alcoholics Anonymous were derived from the following sources:

1. Crim, K., ed. *Abingdon Dictionary of Living Religions.* Nashville, Tenn.: Abingdon, 1981.

2. Kornfeld, J. *The Teachings of Buddha.* Boston and London: Shambhala, 1993.

3. Sangharakshita. *A Guide to the Buddhist Path.* Birmingham, Ala.: Windhorse Publications, 1990.

4. Meyer, R. E. "The Disease Called Addiction: Emerging Evidence in a 200 Year Old Debate." *The Lancet* 347 (1996): 162–66.

5. Levine, H. G. "The Discovery of Addiction: Changing Conceptions of Habitual Drunkenness in America." *Journal of the Study of Alcohol* 39 (1978): 143–74.

6. Alcoholics Anonymous. *The Big Book: The Basic Text for Alcoholics Anonymous,* 1939.

Currently, the three major approaches to the treatment of craving disorders are:

A. The Minnesota Model, Alcoholics Anonymous, and related twelve-step programs.

B. Methadone for opiate addiction.

C. Blocking agents such as naltrexone and aversive agents such as Antabuse.

7. Cook, C. C. "The Minnesota Model in the Management of Drug and Alcohol Dependency: Miracle, Method, or Myth?" *British Journal of Addiction* 83 (1988): 625–34

8. Cook, C. C. "The Minnesota Model in the Management of Drug and Alcohol Dependency: Miracle, Method, or Myth? Evidence and Conclusions." *British Journal of Addiction* 83 (1988): 735–48.

The four identifiable elements of the Minnesota Model are:

1. Change is the most important principle.

2. Alcoholism is a disease.

3. Only abstinence will lead to improvement of lifestyle.

4. The principles of Alcoholics Anonymous must be followed.

In its simplest form, treatment involves assessment and admission to a residential facility and then progression to aftercare, usually involving attendance at AA or NA, individual and group therapy, and counseling and family therapy.

9. Jaffe, J. H. "Drug Addiction and Drug Abuse." In Goodman and Gillman, eds. *The Pharmacological Basis of Therapeutics, 8th ed.*: 522–73. New York: McGraw-Hill, 1993.

Methadone maintenance was originally based on the hypothesis that the chronic use of opioids alters the brain. Opioids produce a euphoria that for months or even years after withdrawal can cause the addict to experience an "opioid hunger" that can only be relieved by opioids. Our view is that it is the craving brain that persists and that methadone biobalances the brain for this substance.

Giving the patient methadone, a long-lasting opioid preparation, stops this hunger. Not surprisingly, methadone does not prevent alcohol or cocaine abuse, which, for many patients, remains a problem. Methadone maintenance programs explicitly emphasize law-abiding behavior rather than abstinence, and its relative efficiency in reaching its goal with motivated patients is well documented. It may seem paradoxical that giving an opioid stops the hunger, while giving a small amount of alcohol stimulates further drinking. As described earlier, this is due to the biological nature of these two substances. Alcohol raises dopamine with little and late serotonin elevation. Narcotics raise both dopamine and serotonin, biobalancing the brain and causing the activity to stop.

10. Acquas, E., M. Meloni, and G. DiChiara. "Blockade of Delta-Opioid Receptors in the Nucleus Accumbens Prevents Ethanol Induced Stimulation of Dopamine Release." *European Journal of Pharmacology* 230 (1993): 239–41.

11. Volpicelli, J. R., K. L. Clay, N. T. Watson, and C. P. O'Brien. "Naltrexone in the Treatment of Alcoholism: Predicting Response to Naltrexone." *The Journal of Clinical Psychiatry* 56 (1995): 39–44.

Alcohol releases dopamine by stimulating the delta opioid receptors in the brain. These receptors are activated by both drugs and pleasurable pattern recognition processes that release internal substances called endorphins. Naltrexone, a blocking agent, prevents the ethanol-induced dopamine release from the nucleus accumbens. Therefore, it can prevent a craving response for alcohol by inhibiting the rise in dopamine in the nucleus accumbens. Based on these observations, studies were undertaken that have shown that naltrexone is an effective pharmacologic treatment for alcohol dependence. It effectively reduces the rate of relapse and the level of craving for alcohol. Through personal observations, we have found that naltrexone is useful in certain eating disorders as well.

12. Rall, T. W. "Hypnotics and Sedatives: Ethanol." In Goodman and Gilman, eds. *The Pharmacological Basis of Therapeutics, 8th ed.*: 345–82. New York: McGraw-Hill, 1993.

Finally, for the motivated drinker, aversive therapy with Antabuse can be useful. Antabuse is not a cure for alcoholism; it merely affords the individual a crutch by which the sincere desire to stop drinking is fortified. If a person ingests alcohol within several days of taking Antabuse, his blood acetaldehyde rapidly rises to five to ten times that of a nontreated individual, producing an acetaldehyde syndrome. Flushing, breathing difficulties, nausea, vomiting, weakness, and dizziness are a few of the unpleasant symptoms that develop. After thirty minutes to several hours, the effects wear off and the exhausted individual may sleep for many hours.

CHAPTER 5

By biobalancing the brain, that is, raising the dopamine and the serotonin, we prevent perceptions from producing a craving response. By increasing the serotonin and decreasing the sensitivity of the nucleus accumbens, the craving brain is corrected, and the craving response cannot develop. Both ways of stopping the craving response require that serotonin be elevated.

If we can raise serotonin, it might be possible, over the long term, to decrease the sensitivity of the nucleus accumbens by decreasing the pattern recognition process and raising dopamine. The decrease in pattern recognition of environmental stressors produced by higher serotonin would not only reduce stress, it might also allow for a rise in dopamine in a brain no longer experiencing these stressful patterns. In other words, raising serotonin may have two salutory effects. Also, by decreasing the perception of stress, glucocorticoids will return to normal. As a consequence, there should be a decrease in the sensitivity of the nucleus accumbens. These concepts provide a mechanism for the effectiveness of neurotherapy (see below).

1. Bujatti, M., and P. Riederer. "Serotonin, Noradrenaline, Dopamine Metabolites in Transcendental Meditation Technique." *Journal of Neural Transmission* 39 (1976): 257–67.

2. Benson, H. *The Relaxation Response.* New York: William Morrow, 1975.

3. Gelderloos, P., K. G. Walton, D. W. Orme-Johnson, and C. N. Alexander. "Effectiveness of the Transcendental Meditation Program in Preventing and Treating Substance Misuse: A Review." *International Journal of Addiction* 26 (1991): 293–95.

The craving response and the craving brain appear to be helped by transcendental meditation (TM). The modern version by Benson is called the relaxation response. It requires repetitive processes. The physiologic effects on metabolism, breathing, skin resistance, brain waves, and the cardiovascular system are exactly the opposite of those identified with the efforts to meet the demands of stress. The reduction of glucocorticoids after TM is connected with increases in serotonin. The results of TM on craving disorders seem to be positive. As Gelderloos concludes, meditation programs simultaneously address several factors underlying chemical dependence, providing not only immediate relief from distress but long-range improvements in well-being, self-esteem, and personal empowerment as well. Acupuncture apparently produces similar results.

4. Cheng, R. S., and B. Pomeranz. "Monoaminergic Mechanism of Electroacupuncture Analgesia." *Brain Research* 215 (1981): 77–92.

5. Smith, M. O., and I. Khan. "An Acupuncture Program for the Treatment of Drug-Addicted Persons." *Bulletin of Narcotics* 40 (1988): 35–41.

6. Gogek, E. B. "The Dry Drunk Syndrome: Subtype of Depression." *American Journal of Psychiatry* 151 (1994): 947–48.

Attending Alcoholics Anonymous can raise serotonin. As Gogek describes, the lay term "dry drunk" refers to the dysphoria experienced by an individual who has stopped drinking. The symptoms reported include feeling deeply depressed, feeling very tired, agitated physical activity, poor concentration, hopelessness, and thoughts of suicide. Involvement in Alcoholics Anonymous appeared to alleviate many of these symptoms.

We have described this dysphoria in Chapter 3 as a low-dopamine, low-serotonin landscape. The ability to raise serotonin by attendance at Alcoholics Anonymous may be similar to the indirect and direct effects that drugs like Prozac have on the tonic dopamine landscape. Like Prozac, Alcoholics Anonymous must be able to raise both dopamine and serotonin to explain the observed effects. (See Cloninger, Chapter 3, reference 9.)

7. Tanda, G., E. Carboni, R. Frau, and G. DiChiara. "Increase in Extracellular Dopamine in the Prefrontal Cortex: A Trait of Drugs with Antidepressant Potential?" *Psychopharmacology* 115 (1994): 285–88.

This also explains why attendance at Alcoholics Anonymous is so important. Just as with medication, meditation, and acupuncture, the serotonin level cannot be sustained if not regularly attended to. Those fortunate enough to decrease the stress in their lives may be able to forgo continuing treatment because their nucleus accumbens are no longer as sensitive. These individuals must be very cautious, however, because new stressors may trigger the return of the craving brain.

8. Marlatt, G. A. "Cue Exposure and Relapse Prevention in the Treatment of Addictive Behaviors." *Addictive Behaviors* 15 (1990): 395–99.

While not directly related to biobalancing the brain, the pattern recognition and response process could also be disrupted if we somehow extinguish the conditioned response. Most of the research in this field is based on the assumption that repeated exposure to drug-taking cues (e.g., drug paraphernalia, alcoholic beverages, cigarette smoke) without the reward will eventually lead to extinction of the craving response. This technique seems to be modestly effective. Problems in applying exposure techniques to the management of addiction exist. Extinction and habituation of responses to drug cues or drug aftereffects are often unstable and strongly dependent on the context.

9. Tobena, A., A. Fernandez-Teruel, R. M. Escorihuela, J. F. Nuñez, A. Zapata, A. P. Ferre, and R. Sanchez. "Limits of Habituation and Extinction: Implications for Relapse Prevention Programs in Addiction." *Drug and Alcohol Dependence* 32 (1993): 209–17.

Several strategies are suggested for improving the stability of extinction of the craving response. Patients should be warned about the episodic resurgence of unexpected urges or cravings that can be precipitated by conditioned contexts. The behavioral chains involved in self-administering drugs ought to be incorporated into cue exposure treatments. The issue of reinstatement as described earlier must be considered. For true extinction, the conditioned stimulus, the thought of alcohol and the presentation of alcohol, must be presented independently. Only then can there be true extinction of the conditioned response. These ideas are still in their infancy and this type of research has not yet been done.

10. Clemens, B. "Dopamine Agonist Treatment of Self-Induced Pattern-Sensitive Epilepsy: A Case Report." *Epilepsy Research* 2 (1988): 340–43.

Raising the brain dopamine and serotonin and biobalancing the brain to treat an unusual addictive disorder was discussed in a short communication by Clemens. This interesting paper describes a case that precisely follows our general theory. The case report is included:

As a complication of pertussis vaccination, a five-month-old infant developed seizures and EEG abnormalities. In addition to spontaneous generalized seizures, at the age of four he developed excessive pattern sensitivity. The visual fixation on checks, stripes, and angles of any size and direction led immediately to generalized seizures. Many irregular patterns such as highlighted foliage and patched surfaces had the same effect. After perceiving his own ability to induce the cloudy state, he displayed an irresistible urge to search for patterns. As a consequence, any pastime in sunlight became impossible because of a series of self-induced seizures.

On admission, he was 5.5 years old, but his cognitive and motor development was clearly retarded. In an acute experiment, apomorphine [which raises dopamine in the brain] was given. This was tried because of the success of this drug in stopping the seizures induced by flickering lights. Based on the results obtained, bromocriptine [which also raises dopamine] was added to the previous medication (valproate and carbamazepine). Although the search for patterns continued, pattern sensitivity decreased. Self-induced seizures became rare, but did not cease. Fenfluramine, which raises serotonin, was then added. Within a few days, the boy was unable to induce seizures, even by long-lasting fixation on previously highly effective patterns. After some weeks, looking for patterns became more and more rare. Due to long lasting seizure control and the lack of pathological reinforcement, his interest turned from seizures to his environment. He was educated at a special school.

Our interpretation is that due to a low serotonin state combined with a sensitive nucleus accumbens, he became addicted to biobalancing his brain by first raising his dopamine with fixation on patterns, and then having his serotonin raised by the seizure. In effect, he was addicted to seizures. We speculate that the apomorphine and the subsequent bromocriptine (which raises dopamine) stabilized the patterns of his visual input and stopped the "flickering" of these patterns which led to the seizures. The fenfluramine raised serotonin and the brain became biobalanced. He lost his craving response.

11. Weintraub, M. "Long-term Weight Control Study: Conclusions." *Clinical Pharmacology and Therapeutics* 51 (1992): 642–46.

This landmark study showed that, by providing medications that would elevate both serotonin and dopamine, patients had their appetitive drive reduced, lost weight, and maintained that weight loss.

12. Hitzig, P. "Combined Dopamine and Serotonin Agonists: A Synergistic Approach to Alcoholism and Other Addictive Behaviors." *Maryland Medical Journal* 42 (1993): 153–56.

13. Hitzig, P. "Combined Serotonin and Dopamine Indirect Agonists Correct Alcohol Craving and Alcohol-Associated Neuroses." *Journal of Substance Abuse Treatment* 11 (1994): 489–90.

The use of these medications in the treatment of substance abuse was first reported by Hitzig. In his studies, there was a profound and long-lasting decrease in alcohol and cocaine craving and neurotic symptomatology in an open trial. In addition to the cessation of craving, other behavioral issues also improved. Somaticism, obsessional-compulsive behavior, depression, anxiety, hostility, and phobias appeared to be helped by this treatment.

CHAPTER 6

1. Selye, H. *The Stress of Life*. New York: McGraw-Hill, 1978.

Here again we see Selye's genius. He recognized that a terrain could be changed not just by adaptation, but by physical substances such as drugs. His term *heterostasis* reflects his appreciation of the need to distinguish this state from the homeostatic state which is set and maintained by the brain's inherent biology. He defines heterostasis as

the establishment of a new steady state by treatment with agents which stimulate the physiologic adaptive mechanisms. Heterostasis depends upon treatment with artificial remedies which have no direct curative action. . . . The most salient difference between homeostasis and heterostasis is that the former maintains a normal steady state by physiologic means, whereas the latter resets the thermostat of resistance to a heightened defensive capacity by artificial interventions from the outside.

It is important to remember that a heterostasis reverts back to its original homeostatic position after the drug is removed. We would like to expand the definition of heterostasis to include that state maintained by a psychological chronic stressor. Adaptation to this stressor produces a heterostasis.

How does a stressor alter the brain? While the exact mechanisms remain unclear, we are able to understand what happens by examining the systems which are activated. The hypothalamus is the central orchestrator.

2. Herman, J. P., C. M. -F. Prewitt, W. E. Cullinan. "Neuronal Circuit Regulation of the Hypothalamic-Pituitary-Adrenocortical (HPA) Stress Axis." *Critical Reviews in Neurobiology* 10, nos. 3 and 4 (1996): 371–94.

The HPA axis is the primary modulator of the adrenal glucocorticoid stress response. Activation of this system occurs by the way of a discrete set of neurons (the paraventricular nucleus) in the hypothalamus. This nucleus appears to be affected by multiple sources, including (1) the brainstem amines (such as dopamine, serotonin, and norepinephrine) as well as peptides (such as enkephalins, somatostatin and Substance P), and (2) indirect input from limbic-system-associated regions such as the prefrontal cortex, hippocampus, and amygdala. Severe systemic stressors appear to be able to trigger this system directly. In contrast, stressors requiring interpretation with respect to previous experience (processed stressors) reach the hypothalamus via multisynaptic pathways. Processed stressors require interaction with the homeostatic landscape prior to promoting a response. These stressors are keyed to the survival importance for the organism, just as systemic stressors are. The release of glucocorticoids by the adrenal gland not only affects peripheral organs but, through widespread receptors in the brain, the functioning of central regulatory systems.

Psychological functioning appears to be homeostatically regulated.

3. Williams, D. E., and J. K. Thompson. "Biology and Behavior: A Setpoint Hypothesis of Psychological Functioning." *Behavior Modification* 17, no. 1 (1993): 43–57.

These authors contend that psychological function has a substantial basis in physiology with a specified (inherent) level of responsiveness and a surrounding bandwidth of typical behavior for a given individual. Thus, psychological function may be described from a homeostatic perspective. In short, past behavior is the best predictor of future behavior because the brain returns to a preset behavioral repertoire. The idea here is that there are physiological mechanisms in place, by and large, to maintain a stable personality structure. It is of immense importance, however, that through certain types of intervention the bandwidth and the setpoint can be altered.

4. van der Kolk, B. A., and R. E. Fisler. "The Biologic Basis of Posttraumatic Stress Disorder." *Primary Care* 20, no. 2 (1993): 417–32.

In 1945 Kardiner and Spiegel stated that a "traumatic neurosis (PTSD) is an enduring physical sensation. It outlives every intermediary accommodative device and persists in the chronic forms." The key question is what is the nature of this process which makes it persistent and resistant to change? These researchers feel that this persistence is due to a conditioned autonomic arousal and that the terrain is never at rest. Indeed, one can speculate that the disorder worsens over time because other stimuli can become associated with the trauma and produce a hyperarousal response. Increased levels of norepinephrine and CRF as well as alterations in cortisol levels are most commonly seen. A new landscape is formed. This new steady state functioning can be observed in the EEG as rhythms which are different from those observed in individuals who do not exhibit this disorder. To appreciate these changes, we must first understand how these rhythms are generated.

5. Nunez, Paul L., ed. *Neocortical Dynamics and Human EEG Rhythms*. New York: Oxford University Press, 1995.

This mathematically daunting text provides a tentative theoretical framework for neocortical function, cognitive processing, and the EEG. Despite the fact that not all the information discussed here is accessible, even to most neuroscientists, there are lively discussions of mind-brain systems, neural networks, and what makes a theory. From our viewpoint, Silberstein's chapter entitled "Neuromodulation of Neocortical Dynamics" is especially interesting. According to Silberstein, as dopamine and noradrenaline increase there is a shift from global resonance modes (low frequency waves) to local resonance modes (high frequency waves). Serotonin appears to do the opposite. Thus, dopamine and noradrenaline increase frequency of the EEG and serotonin decreases frequency. In terms of associative processing, local groups (high frequency rhythms) may reflect strong (and anatomically nearby) associations and lower frequency may represent pathways to looser associations (anatomically further away). Very low frequency may reflect free association.

Generating alpha may increase serotonin concentrations in several areas of the brain, most importantly the limbic system. The consequence may be a decreased reactivity of the stress system.

6. Neidermeyer, E., and F. Lopes Da Silva. *Electro-encephalography: Basic Principles, Clinical Applications, and Related Fields*. 4th ed. Baltimore: Williams & Wilkins, 1999.

Considered to be the definitive introductory text, this book explores the origins and meaning of what is observed on the EEG. From chapters on cellular substrates of brain rhythms to brain mapping, we are treated to state-of-the-art information. It is noteworthy that the text describes much of what we know as only a hypothesis.

There are many features in this text not discussed in *The Craving Brain*, such as synchrony, event related potentials, and so on, which make EEG an incredibly rich, complex, and fascinating field.

A simple schema for brain rhythms is outlined below.

Beta. Irregular waves of 14–30 Hz. Beta waves are involved with thinking functions.

Alpha. A regular rhythmic wave of 8–12 Hz. Associated with relaxed wakefulness. It appears to be associated with a broadening of associative processes.

Theta. A regular rhythm of 3–7 Hz. Associated with hypnogogic imagery and a reverie state. During high amplitude theta rhythm, visualization of alcohol rejection scenes appears to be useful in the treatment of alcoholism.

Delta. A large amplitude, low frequency wave between .5 and 3.5 Hz. Found in normal deep sleep beyond dreams.

In alcoholism, abnormal brain waves have been documented.

7. Volavka, J., V. Pollock, W. F. Gabrielli, and S. A. Mednick. "The EEG in Persons at Risk for Alcoholism." *Recent Developments in Alcoholism* 3 (1985): 21–36.

Investigations have described EEG features of human alcoholism. Several groups that have studied the sons of alcoholics and chronic alcoholics have demonstrated that even after prolonged abstinence, alcoholics have lower levels of alpha on their background EEG.

Research has shown that many different disorders can be understood in terms of their EEG signatures.

8. Hughes, J. R., and E. R. John. "Conventional and Quantitative Electroencephalography in Psychiatry." *Journal of Neuropsychiatry and Clinical Neuroscience* 11, no. 2 (1999): 190–201.

These authors state that for an individual, the electrical activity of each brain region is homeostatically regulated, resulting in a predictable frequency composition of the EEG. This is called QEEG, quantitative electroencephalography. By studying many individuals, replicated normative databases have been obtained. In subjects with psychiatric disorders, high proportions of abnormal findings have been reported on QEEG. Dementia, learning and attention disorders, and mood disorders are all discernible. Interestingly, abnormalities related to schizophrenia and substance abuse are not readily observable. This may be due to their many sub-types.

8a. Thatcher, R. W. "EEG Database-guided Neurotherapy." In Evans and Abarbanel, eds. *Introduction to Quantitative EEG and Neurofeedback*: 29–66. San Diego: Academic Press, 1999.

This chapter, also written by a leader in this field, describes the difficulties in preparation of normative databases. The key elements include:

1. An uneventful prenatal, perinatal, and postnatal period.

2. No disorders of consciousness.

3. No head injury with cerebral symptoms.

4. No history of central nervous system diseases.

5. No seizure disorder.

6. No developmental deviation.

After the preparation of this database, the issue of therapy design and evaluation is discussed. These two landmark articles describe a new powerful tool for the diagnosis and treatment of brain dysfunction.

It is worthwhile looking at these significant rhythms more closely.

9. Markand, N. O. "Alpha Rhythms." *Journal of Clinical Neurophysiology* 7, no. 2 (1990): 163–89.

There are many interesting features of alpha rhythms. There is controversy concerning the locations at which alpha rhythms can be observed. Some scientists believe they are generated only in the occiput, others feel that they are found over the entire skull. Alpha rhythm is replaced, to a varying extent, by a higher frequency beta rhythm with eye opening and, to a lesser extent, by auditory, tactile, or other sensory stimuli or by sustained elevated mental processes (arithmetic solving). The frequency of the alpha rhythm changes markedly throughout childhood, but it becomes quite stable after the age of twenty years.

The amount of alpha rhythm and its response to eye opening appears to be unique to the individual. It is felt by many (not all) to be generated in the cortex by multiple, small generators of alpha rhythm.

10. Sadato, N., S. Nakamura, T. Oohasi, E. Nishina, Y. Fuwamoto, A. Waku, and Y. Yonekura. "Neural Networks

for the Generation and Suppression of Alpha Rhythm: A PET Study." *Neuroreport* 9 (1998): 893–97.

These workers investigated positron emission tomography (a measure of blood flow) to study the neuronal systems used in the generation of alpha rhythm. A positive correlation was found for the right pons and right midbrain. The hypothalamus, thalamus, the amygdala, the basal prefrontal cortex, and the insula (which has extensive connections with limbic, paralimbic, olfactory, gustatory, and autonomic structures) on the right side of the brain were also activated. Mania, anger, dread, panic, suicidal feelings, and explosive behavior lessen with the calming of the right hemisphere during neurofeedback training. Alpha rhythm appears to reflect the activity of those parts of the brain involved in the stress response and in emotionally mediated states.

11. Vinogradova, O. S. "Expression, Control, and Functional Significance of the Neuronal Theta Rhythm." *Progress in Neurobiology* 45 (1995): 523–83.

The function and modulation of the slow sinusoidal wave of 3–7Hz. (theta) generated in the hippocampus, felt to be the seat for memory formation, has been extensively studied. Acetylcholine and serotonin are thought to be involved in the modulation of the theta rhythm. Acetylcholine increases both the frequency and the amplitude, while serotonin decreases both. It is suggested that the theta rhythm has a double function in information processing. Theta appears to facilitate and prolong the action of the stimuli entering the hippocampus in phase with concomitantly triggered theta (filtering in), and it prevents the admission of signals appearing during on-going theta triggered by a previous event (filtering out), eliminating interference during processing and registration of information. Thus, the theta rhythm may be regarded as a mechanism of selective attention and a prerequisite for memory formation. Theta rhythm may also be the state in which visualizations (see below, ref. 13) exert their power.

Some individuals in the neurofeedback community feel that there is a healthy theta and an unhealthy theta. Healthy theta leads to retrieving old memories and consolidation of new memory traces. Unhealthy theta appears to be a dissociative state, where the individual becomes confused and disoriented. It is possible that these two theta rhythms are due to differential acetylcholine input into the hippocampus and cortex.

The history of the EEG and its relationship to neurofeedback is also fascinating.

12. Berger, H. "Uber das Elektrenkephalogramm des Menschen." *Arch. Psychiatry. Nervenkr.* 87 (1929): 527–70.

Berger was the first to describe alpha rhythm. It is of historical interest that Berger declined to have the rhythm he identified named after him.

12a. Budzynski, T. H. "From EEG to Neurofeedback." In
Evans and Abarbanel, eds. *Introduction to Quantitative
EEG and Neurofeedback:* 65–79. San Diego: Academic
Press, 1999.

This wonderful short chapter describes the ups and
downs of research in the early days of clinical neurofeedback.

The application of neurofeedback to the problem of alcoholism has been outlined by Pensiton and Kulkowsky.

13. Peniston, E. G., and P. J. Kulkosky. "Alpha-theta brain
wave training and beta-endorphin levels in alcoholics."
Alcoholism: Clinical and Experimental Research 13
(1989): 271–79.

———."Alcoholic personality and alpha-theta brain wave
training." *Medical Psychotherapeutics* 3 (1990): 37–55.

———."Alpha-theta brain wave neurofeedback therapy
for Vietnam veterans with combat related posttraumatic
stress disorder." *Medical Psychotherapeutics* 4 (1991):
47–60.

These papers will assuredly provide the basis of future
research for years to come. Currently, their protocol has subjects trained five times a week. Training includes thermal
biofeedback followed by thirty-minute sessions of alpha-theta
training. Subjects were instructed to close their eyes and con-

struct visualized abstinence/alcohol rejection scenes and scenes of the normalization of their personality. The control group of alcoholics showed a significant increase in beta-endorphin (such an increase implies greater stress) after standard medical treatment and abstinence. The lack of corresponding increase in beta-endorphin in alcoholics receiving neurofeedback suggests that the deliberate application of this therapy provides a way of preventing the maladaptive stress of abstinence which may ultimately lead to relapse. Indeed, in this paper, after a thirteen-month followup, eight out of ten individuals remained sober whereas eight of the ten control patients were readmitted for detoxification. In addition, depression improved and personality factors, as described by the Milion Clinical Multiaxial Inventory, also improved. The personality changes reported correspond to being more warmhearted, more intelligent, more emotionally stable, more socially bold, more relaxed, and more satisfied.

The biological framework for neurofeedback and the regulatory systems are described in two articles by leaders in this field.

14. Othmer, S., O. F. Othmer, and David Kaiser. "EEG Biofeedback: an emerging model for its global efficiency." In Evans and Abarbanel, eds., *Introduction to Quantitative EEG and Neurofeedback*: 243–310. San Diego: Academic Press, 1999.

This creative model described by Othmer, Othmer, and Kaiser

> treats the brain as a self-regulatory control system, and much of psychopathology will be seen in terms of specific failure modes of such a control system. It will be referred to as the dysregulation model. *Much of the basic regulatory activity of the central nervous system manifests itself in rhythmic EEG activity.* EEG biofeedback appeals to that regulatory machinery by operant conditoning on its rhythmic manifestations. EEG is therefore a regulatory challenge to which the system responds by becoming more robust as a control system and more capable of returning to homeostasis.

In short, these authors assert that the functional deficits underlying much psychopathology are often largely remediable by means of operant conditioning of the brain waves as recorded in the EEG. This training alters the mechanisms by which these rhythmic processes are established and maintained.

First, it is unclear to us why we should call this operant conditoning. Operant conditioning is state-dependent, where an arbitrary response (pushing a button, avoiding an object, or increasing alpha amplitude) is reinforced—that is, it is followed by the presentation of a reward. In the case of neurofeedback, the reward is to sustain a sound or move objects on a screen. Unlike systemic rewards (food when hungry or the avoidance of an electrical shock) which alter biological systems (less hunger and less fear), it is unclear how operant conditioning occurs in neurofeedback where a visual or audio signal is reinforced. There is no removal of a specific pain. Nothing is biobalanced (e.g., no reward); therefore, there is no operant conditioning. A rat that is not hungry will not push a lever for more food. However, we can look at this process in another way.

14a. Abarbanel, A. "The Neural Underpinnings of Neurofeedback Training." In Evans and Abarbanel, eds. *Introduction to Quantitative EEG and Neurofeedback:* 311–40. San Diego: Academic Press, 1999.

This author suggests that during neurofeedback, the patient learns to exert neuromodulatory control over the circuitry system mediating the attentional process. Over time, biological mechanisms consolidate an optimization of attentional processes. This is called long-term potentiation. In terms of network theory, it can be said that during neurofeedback the system is neuromodulated into an attractor state, a stable point of equilibrium for the system. At this level of explanation, one can analogize what happens in neurofeedback to learning a motor task, like riding a bicycle. Practice over time automatizes the skill.

To us, it seems that neurofeedback works because we produce a neohomeostatic state by reducing the effect that stessors have on the stress system. It is driven in essence by:

(1) decreasing associative processing (e.g., a jingle of ice cubes may not produce the thought of alcohol) and (2) decreasing the responsiveness of the system so that the stimulus can not breach the threshold to craving.

This idea combines the dysregulation model (in our approach, however, it is not the individual regulatory systems which are affected; rather, it is the stress system which secondarily affects the other regulatory systems) and non-associative learning (bike riding, walking, ice skating, etc.), through which this is accomplished. Thus, once a neohomeostasis is produced it can self sustain and improve our ability to reduce maladaptive stress, exactly the opposite of that which occurs in PTSD, which worsens over time.

Several groups have reported long-term benefits of neurofeedback. Our own experience with alcohol addicted individuals is consistent with these reports.

15. White, N. E. "Theories of the of Alpha-theta training for multiple disorders." In Evans and Abarbanel, eds. *Introduction to Quantitative EEG and Neurofeedback:* 341–67. San Diego: Academic Press, 1999.

15b. Fahrion, S. L., E. D. Walters, C. Lolafaye, and T. Allen. "Alterations in EEG amplitude, personality factors, and brain electrical mapping after alpha-theta brainwave training: A controlled case study of an alcoholic in recovery." *Alcoholism: Clinical and Experimental Research* 16, no. 3 (1992): 547–55.

16. Processes which leave permanent changes on the landscape appear to occur during brain maturation, as well as in extreme emotional states. There is an immense amount of literature on this topic. Lack of nurturing, abandonment, and physical and mental abuse all alter the landscape permanently, especially in the young. Neurofeedback, when appropriately applied, appears to open the window to the landscape and to produce a neohomeostasis, thereby allowing for a happier, fuller life.

CHAPTER 7

1. Robins, L. N., D. H. Davis, and D. N. Nurco. "How Permanent Was Vietnam Drug Addiction?" *American Journal of Public Health,* 64 (1974): 38–43.

If addiction and the risk of addiction rises with chronic inescapable stress, what would happen if we removed the chronic stress? Would the addiction stop?

During the summer and fall of 1971, drug use by United States servicemen in Vietnam had, by all estimates, reached epidemic proportions. Starting in

June 1971, the military screened urine of returning servicemen for drugs just prior to their scheduled departure from Vietnam. In September 1971, 5 percent of all urine of Army servicemen tested indicated drug use, despite common knowledge that such testing would be done and would result, if positive, in a six- or seven-day delay in departure from Vietnam.

At this time, American troop strength was being rapidly reduced, returning thousands of men to the United States each month. The Armed Forces, the Veteran's Administration, and civilian drug treatment centers were concerned that the arrival of these men might tax existing drug treatment centers. There was also concern about how drug use would affect veterans' abilities to get and hold jobs, as well as their chances of becoming involved in criminal activities, especially with their knowledge of advanced weapons. To evaluate these concerns, and to learn how many would require treatment and social services, the White House Special Action Office for Drug Abuse Prevention carried out a follow-up study of these men.

Among returnees in the general sample, 43 percent reported having used narcotics in Vietnam. Of that 43 percent, almost half felt that they were addicted. After return from Vietnam, not only did the number of users drop dramatically, from 43 percent to 10 percent, but the proportion who remained addicted dropped. Only 7 percent of those reporting having used any narcotics reported that they had been addicted since their return.

For those who continued to use narcotics after Vietnam, there was more regular use leading to more addiction among men after their exposure to Vietnam. Thus post-Vietnam narcotic use was more serious than pre-Vietnam use, even if not more common. Nonetheless, heavy or addictive use was still much rarer than might have been expected based on the high recidivism rates reported for treated civilian addicts. There have been no studies of addict populations in this country that show anything like the 95 percent remission rate after ten months, which is what a drop from 20 percent to 1 percent after Vietnam suggests. The removal of chronic inescapable stress (among other things) allowed the Vietnam veteran to alter his landscape.

2. An interesting and impressive example of biobalance can be seen in the work done by the Doe Fund. This organization founded by George and Harriet McDonald brings homeless addicts into their program, houses them, and puts them to work. There is inhouse counseling and each individual is responsible for his area. This simple model, a home and work environment that provides for effort and rewards, has been remarkably successful. Though most men clean streets, others

learn about construction. They are randomly tested to determine drug use and any infraction is dealt with by dismissal from the program. Many individuals eventually leave, get jobs, and return to the community free of their addiction. The overall success rate is such that New York City has awarded the Doe Fund a twenty-year contract. Other cities have used this model with similar positive results.

POSTFACE

During the past four years I have medically biobalanced almost three thousand individuals and have witnessed many remarkable things. Probably the most notable is how consistently the craving response can be abolished. For most, this effect is profound and prolonged; for some, the brain adapts and occasional cravings return; and for a few, the cravings return quickly and appear untouched by medical therapy. Our current research is directed at exploring new ways to sustain an individual in a biobalanced state and, we hope, without the use of medications.

For those who have not experienced an addiction, it seems incomprehensible that such behavior cannot be stopped by exercising willpower. It can't. I have been impressed that the power of the mind is no match for the relentless power Nature has provided to ensure our survival. A craving brain will eventually lead to addictive behavior. By biobalancing the brain, we can prevent a craving response. No craving, no addiction.

Addiction and its consequent effects on our lives are well known: families are destroyed, careers ruined, and fortunes lost. Its effects outside the immediate family are also devastating. Every day we read of strangers killed by intoxicated individuals, and innocent bystanders injured by those seeking money to feed their addictions. There is also the huge societal cost of caring for those addicted and the related diseases this behavior produces. The addict poses problems for the family, the local neighborhood, and the community at large.

To heal addiction, therefore, heals the world.

POSTFACE TO THE SECOND EDITION

Neurofeedback and other neurotherapies will soon take their place along with psychotherapy and pharmacotherapy as one of the three major pillars for the treatment of mental illnesses, including alcoholism. For many, the craving brain can be healed by decreasing the sensitivity of the stress system. For others, an underlying brain dysregulation (such as bipolar disorder or ADD) also needs to be treated. For still others, the environment needs to be changed. Nonetheless, it seems that addiction is a solvable problem when approached from a biological perspective. **It is not the drug: it is the CRAVING BRAIN**. Heal this, and we end addiction.

GLOSSARY

Acetylcholine. A neurotransmitter and neuromodulator whose origin lies in the midbrain and which sends neurons to the hippocampus and cortex.

Adaptation. The process by which the regulator systems handle stressors. According to Hans Selye, there are three stages of biological reactions to a stressor. There is the alarm reaction, the stage of resistance, and the stage of exhaustion. It is in the stage of resistance where the body tries to restore homeostasis by altering related symptoms.

Addiction. A strong dependence, both physiological and emotional, on the use of a chemical substance or activity.

The consequence of a craving response when the craved object produces physiological changes in the brain associated with tolerance and withdrawal.

Agonist. A drug that facilitates the action of a neurotransmitter.

Anticipatory phase of goal-driven behaviors. The time when the survival system drives the animal to seek a way of biobalancing its brain. Thinking about the desired object as well as being motivated to obtain it are processes going on at this time. Dopamine rises in the brain and nucleus accumbens during this phase.

Arousal. A pattern of measurable physiological changes (including increased heart rate, tense muscles, secretion of certain hormones) that puts us on alert. This state of being can arise from a thought, an object, or a sensory input.

Backfield. Sensory input that is not focused upon. The backfield and forefield can change quickly. Driving a car provides an excellent example. We can follow the car in front of us as a forefield process and have the other cars and the scenery in the backfield. Signs along the road can be forefield or backfield, depending upon if you know where you're going or you're trying to find your way.

Biobalance. To alter information processing such that a pattern recognition process cannot produce a conditioned rise of dopamine in the nucleus accumbens.

Biobalanced. A high-dopamine, high-serotonin state in

which the pattern recognition process does not motivate behavior. It is the state after the survival system has just completed its motivated task. It produces a feeling of contentment, without conscious awareness of need for more. We are unbiobalanced when we become aware of a need.

Compulsive behavior. The strong impulse to do something contrary to one's will. A stereotyped repetitive action that a person feels impelled to perform. Obsessively washing hands, drinking alcohol, exercising, and gambling are some examples.

Conditioned response. According to Pavlov, the learned or acquired response to a conditioned stimulus (e.g., to a stimulus that did not evoke the response originally).

Conscious. The memories, feelings, and drives of which the individual is aware right now. This process, often requiring a focus of the sensory apparatus, remains one of the unsolved mysteries of the human condition.

Corticotrophin releasing factor (CRF). A substance released by the hypothalamus which causes the release of ACTH and glucocorticoids. It has other effects as well since receptors are found throughout the brain, particularly in the limbic system.

Craving brain. The state of the brain when its landscape is primed for a craving response, exhibiting low serotonin with a highly sensitive nucleus accumbens.

Craving response. The mental and behavioral consequence of a pattern recognition process that raises dopamine on the nucleus accumbens on a landscape of low serotonin. An extreme biological response, it renders the mind unable to control the behavioral component.

Cue. A stimulus or pattern of stimuli capable of eliciting a particular action or set of actions.

Denial. A mechanism by which unacceptable impulses or ideas are not allowed into full awareness. The inability to bring to the forefield an idea that appears to be self-evident.

Dopamine. A neurochemical that acts as both a neurotransmitter and a neuromodulator to increase salience and control motor action.

Dysphoria. A feeling of dejection, unhappiness, and dissatisfaction with life or self, often manifested as underestimation of self on any or every level.

EEG (Electroencephalography). A technique that measures brainwaves generated by the brain's activities.

Estrogen. A female sex hormone that regulates sexual behavior, promotes the growth of secondary sex characteristics, and is essential in maintaining pregnancy.

Extinction. The gradual disappearance of a conditioned response due to either a lack of reinforcement, aversive therapy, or a prolonged absence of activity.

Extracellular. Referring to what's happening outside the cell. An increase in the extracellular concentration of a substance between two neurons suggests that that substance is transmitting or modulating neural function.

Fenfluramine. A drug that acts as both a chemical releaser and an uptake inhibitor of serotonin.

Field. The sum of the forefield and the backfield.

5-HIAA. Breakdown product of serotonin, 5-*h*ydroxy*i*ndole-*a*cetic *a*cid.

Forefield. Where the focus of sensory input lies when it is brought to consciousness.

General adaptation syndrome. A pattern of responses to stressful circumstances that consists of alarm, resistance, and exhaustion stages. According to Hans Seyle, it is the body's response to a stressor rather than the stressor itself that is responsible for disease.

Genetic. Produced or predetermined by a gene or a combination of genes.

Glucocorticoids. A group of hormones involved with the stress response that has anti-inflammatory properties. They also sensitize the nucleus accumbens to stimulation by patterns.

Heterostasis. A new state generated by either drugs or a chronic inescapable stressor of the mind. The landscape reverts back to its homeostatic levels after the drug is removed or the inescapable stressor is removed.

Hippocampus. A structure deep inside the brain that is believed to be where memory and information processing are modulated.

Homeostasis. The body's tendency to maintain the conditions of its internal environment by various forms of self-regulation. The sum total of all survival systems in maintaining the body during times of stress.

Incentive. Any object or end that exists in the external environment and toward which behavior is directed.

Inescapable stress. A problem for which the organism can find no solution. No action can alter the situation and there appears to be no way out.

Landscape. The result of the interaction between the terrain and the environment. The landscape is viewed as dynamic and ever-changing while retaining the fundamental aspects of the terrain.

Landscaping. The process by which hormones and environment alter the terrain.

Limbic system. A set of brain structures including a relatively primitive part of the cerebral cortex and parts of the thalamus and hypothalamus. An ancient part of the brain consisting of a group of well-defined neural cellular structures (amygdala, hippocampus, septum, and the nucleus accumbens) that receives sensory input and modulates its affective content. Two major biologic functions, self-preservation and species preservation, are directed from this system. It is involved with the regulation of states of arousal, desire, and motivation, and plays a role in incentive learning.

Mesolimbic dopamine system. A group of cellular structures in the brain, including the limbic system, the nucleus accumbens, and the tegmentum. It is involved in survival activities, motivation, and incentive learning, and regulates the intensity of the survival system.

Naltrexone. A drug that inhibits the effect of morphine and similar opiates and blocks the pain alleviation ascribed to endorphins. It blocks the rise of dopamine in the nucleus accumbens from alcohol, opiates, and, in certain individuals, food cravings.

Neohomeostasis. A new term which describes a new steady state. It is self-sustaining.

Neurochemical. One of over eighty substances like amino acids, proteins, steroids, smaller molecules, and even single elements that affect the functional activity of nerve tissues. Dopamine and serotonin are examples of amino acid–derived neurochemicals. The intestinal hormone cholecystokinin, the small molecule nitrous oxide, the element lithium, and the glucocorticoid cortisol are other examples.

Neurofeedback. A technique utilizing the EEG wherein frequency domains (alpha, beta, theta) are used in such a way as to increase or decrease activity generated by the brain.

Neuromodulator. A neurochemical that alters the threshold to the flow of information, but does not necessarily alter the nature of the signal. It acts like a filtering agent, expanding or contracting the pattern recognition process.

Neurotransmitter. A chemical involved in the transmission of nerve impulses across the synapse from one neuron to another. It alters the frequency and the amplitude of the message being sent and has a short-lived excitatory or inhibitory affect on an adjacent neuron.

Nirvana. An unconditioned state with high dopamine and high serotonin. What we call, in this book, a biobalanced state.

Operant conditioning. A technique wherein a behavior is reinforced through effort and reward or avoidance of punishment.

Opiates. Drugs that induce a dreamy, relaxed state and, in some people, intense feelings of pleasure. They exert their effects by stimulating special receptor sites within the brain. They include heroin, morphine, codeine, and oxycodone.

Pattern. A recognizable part of either the forefield or backfield, it may be either conscious or subconscious. All patterns that are recognized can affect the landscape.

Pattern recognition. The system by which the brain matches sensory input to create a perception.

Perception. The process of identifying, organizing, interpreting, integrating, and retrieving sensory information. The process of becoming aware of one's environment through the senses.

Phasic. The up and down changes in the levels of dopamine and serotonin in response to a pattern recognition process, as occurs in the nucleus accumbens.

Phentermine. A chemical stimulant that, among other things, raises dopamine and probably serotonin.

Predisposition. Partly inherent and partly environmental, it is the critical step before response. Predisposition adds the affective content to perception. Its modulation of perception most often occurs within certain parameters known as the temperament. In this book, predisposition is what we call the landscape.

Preference drinking. A research technique that allows the researcher to breed animals selectively for alcohol preference.

Primal survival systems. A group of systems that provide incentive motivation and satiety for survival. Regulated by the most primitive parts of the brain (for humans, with substantial input from the neocortex), they reflect the survival needs of getting food, having sex, and finding a safe place.

Processed stressor. A stressor that requires evaluation by the neocortex.

Projections. The road map of a particular group of neurons as it courses through the brain.

Response. The result of stimulation in the form of a movement or biological change. It is the final output resulting from the processes of sensation, perception, and predisposition. A response can be behavioral or cognitive, conscious or subconscious, but always affects the landscape.

Salience. Prominent, conspicuous, important, striking.

Seasonal affective disorder. A malady associated with decreased daylight, producing symptoms of depression, increased craving, lethargy, and irritability. This ailment responds to substances that raise serotonin.

Sensation. The experience that occurs when a sense organ is stimulated. A feeling resulting from excitation of parts of the nervous system. Input about the physical world provided by our sensory receptors. Sight, sound, taste, smell, touch, blood pressure, balance, and blood sugar are examples. Internal sensations that are not brought to consciousness are evaluated by the autonomic nervous system, working, in essence, like a subconscious pattern recognition and response system. External sensation begins the process of pattern recognition and response, some of which will reach consciousness.

Serotonin. A neurochemical found in the brain, intestines, and blood that is thought to transmit neural impulses across synapses in the brain and play a role in the regulation of emotion and sleep. It acts as a neuromodulator and decreases salience and dopamine-mediated exploratory behavior.

Stimuli. Any phenomenon that initiates a response or evokes sensory activity. It may be internal or external to an organism and physical or mental in nature. A stimulus can have many pattern recognition connections.

Stress. The result of a stimulus or change in the environment, the consequences of which can be a physiological or psychological response. It can activate regulators locally, such as when the body reacts to a small cut or pinch, or globally, such as when you are worried or very ill.

Subconscious. The state in which mental processes take place without conscious perception on the individual's part. The ability to make subconscious ideas and feelings conscious varies, depending on the degree of distress produced by bringing them to consciousness. This ability is modulated by both serotonin and dopamine.

Survival systems. An arrangement of interactive sets of biochemical reactions that alter the physiological state and help maintain the body's internal milieu in the face of stress. They can produce physiological as well as psychological changes in the organism.

Synaptic connections. Places where neurons meet to exchange information. Interactions can be facilitatory or inhibitory.

Systemic stessor. A physiological stressor. In general these are autonomically regulated by the brainstem, e.g., blood pressure, temperature.

Terrain. The home of what is genetic, essentially one's inherent temperament. Unique as a fingerprint, it is distinguished by broad, stable behavior patterns.

Testosterone. The male hormone which at the onset of puberty involves an increase in muscle mass, aggressiveness, and sexual desires.

Tolerance. With continued use, the person needs more and more of the drug to achieve the same effect.

Tonic. The amount of dopamine and serotonin present on an ongoing basis—the baseline. In (P) rats, for example, the tonic levels of serotonin are low. Individuals can have high, low, or intermediate levels of dopamine and serotonin. The consequences of these levels can be understood in terms of neural processing theory.

Unconditioned response. The response that is elicited by the unconditioned stimulus. An automatic, primitive reflex that does not require learning. Sucking on a nipple, salivation in response to mother's milk, and following a mother's shape (imprinting) are examples.

Withdrawal. The physical and psychological effects of stopping drug use. The physical symptoms depend on the abused substance. Withdrawal from calming agents can lead to seizures. Removal of stimulant medication can produce depression. Abruptly stopping anxiety medication can provoke severe anxiety. Withdrawal from narcotics can produce headaches, abdominal pain, and nausea.

INDEX